women
in search of mission

*A History of the General Conference
Mennonite Women's Organization*

Gladys V. Goering

Faith and Life Press
Newton, Kansas

Library of Congress Catalog Card Number 80-66787
International Standard Book Number 0-87303-062-1
Printed in the United States of America
Copyright © 1980 by Faith and Life Press
718-B Main Street, Newton, Kansas 67114

Design by Gwen Claassen
Printing by Mennonite Press, Inc.

introduction

This is the story of an organization which began in the middle of the nineteenth century with one mission society and grew to include over four hundred groups by 1980. It was an involvement born and nurtured in Mennonite homes. Busy wives and mothers made time for church work in their days already full of bearing and caring for children, undergirding their husbands, canning and sewing and patching. Many of them never traveled far, but their homes offered a welcome for countless guests who enriched their lives and their families. They provided a bridge between home and conference with their open hospitality, and often quite unconsciously opened vistas of conference work for their children.

This is also an account of single women whose devotion and capabilities promoted the work of the church, and who routinely and unselfishly gave hours of extra time.

It began with the unofficial title of "Woman's Work." Considering that the administration of the conference and church rarely included women, this title for the structure which used their talents was quite appropriate. Much of the early activity included sewing, which Mennonite women not only could do but did expertly; and they carried their name proudly through many years, long after the lines between what was woman's work and what was congregational activity were blurred. When the executives first began publishing their efforts through *The Mennonite* and *Der Bote* they chose the headings "Our Woman's Work" and "Die

Frauenecke." Perhaps it would have been better for the organization if their headings had invited greater readership to that which actually involved the whole conference.

For the first thirty years of its existence the missionary association had neither office nor employee. Handwritten letters from friend to friend wrote history on kitchen tables. Only the minutes of the triennial sessions were kept in the early years, but numerous letters record between-sessions excitement and frustration. The correspondence does more than list facts and procedures; it gives a glimpse into the hearts of the pioneers of this organization and those who followed them. The stories are told by the woman who had time to write while her irons were heating on the range, and by the woman who hurriedly jotted down her ideas just before she boarded a plane for a family holiday. Letters from today's Women in Mission added to the picture as they shared their own society histories or their evaluations of this phase of church work.

Although this is a narrative about an organization, in many ways it is the story of all women who were held to the side of congregational involvement and who through plain resolution made a place for their own contributions. Often in this account women showed exemplary Christian devotion and enthusiasm, but occasionally they were more stubborn than the persons whose authority they sometimes found irritating. If there is a single thread woven through this history from the beginning to the present, it is the determination of the Mennonite woman to be part of the mission of the church.

This account tells of ways in which women who belonged to mission groups were an influence on, and were influenced by, the church in which they wanted to be obedient to the call of God as they journeyed from *Woman's Work* to *The Home and Foreign Missionary Association* to *Women's Missionary Association* to *Women in Mission*.

Women's groups were known as societies, *Vereins*, aids, circles, and fellowships. In the interest of simplicity, this history will use the term *society* only. Rather than editorially using the same form of writing names, we have chosen instead to utilize the woman's own way of identifying herself. Sometimes that was as Martha Goerz, sometimes as Mrs. Rudolph Goerz, and sometimes as Martha Goerz (Mrs. R.).

Not every official act of the organization will be recorded in this brief book, nor the names of all who served as its officers or on its committees. Nor could it begin to name all on the home fronts who loyally made the work and outreach possible. Their recognition will have to come in their own knowledge that they were indeed *Women in Mission*.

contents

Susannah Hirschler Haury　　　*Martha Krehbiel Goerz*

Anna Penner Isaac

1 beginnings

The year was 1917, and the General Conference Mennonite Church was meeting in its triennial session at First Mennonite Church in Reedley, California. Three women sat in a car parked on the church grounds. They had just been elected by the conference women as the first Executive Committee of the General Conference women's society, and this was their official meeting.

During the week a sunrise prayer meeting for women was held on the high school lawn. One of the topics they talked about was, How can our societies best conduct their work to really further missions? But the minutes of that meeting do not mention an election.

The women were in charge of an evening mission program, as they had been since the early 1890s, but it is unlikely that they would have had an election there. The "special meeting" they reported later would doubtless have conflicted with the conference business sessions, as in previous years; but the women, and quite a few of the missionaries, left the session to conduct some business of their own. Here the Executive Committee had been elected and the organization was born. When the societies would meet again at the next triennial session, only eleven women could say they had also been present at the organizational meeting. It was an inconspicuous beginning.

More important to the conference was the war in Europe, which cast its shadow even on the group at First Mennonite. When the crown prince of Austria was assassinated in June 1914, the countries of Europe divided into two big camps struggling for power, with Austria and Germany on one side, and England, France, Russia, and Italy on the other. Canada entered the war shortly after England, but enlistment was voluntary until two months before the General Conference met. In April of 1917 the United States declared war on Germany, and Mennonites in both the United States and Canada felt the conflict of conscription which they had sought to escape by emigration. German-Americans, including many Mennonites who had relatives and friends in Europe, were confused about the issues, and there was considerable support for both sides in the war that was supposed to make the world safe for democracy. Mennonite women were responding to the call to "Knit Your Bit" for the boys.

At First Mennonite that August, the brethren were engrossed in what war meant to the conference. Missionaries, especially those in India, were being forced to cancel furloughs because of travel restrictions, and there was tension in the mission areas.

On the home front the draft was of prime importance. Pacifism was facing a severe test. Many papers and reports of that session dealt with the issue of what Christian nonresistance meant. Uneasy about ties with nonpacifists, the conference decided to withdraw from the Federal Council of Churches. Women named in the conference minutes were those in mission work, and none gave any reports personally. Is it possible that in those particularly urgent times one of the motives for the women to organize was that they felt the need to be more than bystanders?

The names of the persons who promoted this cooperative venture are lost in history, but it may have been missionaries in India. Mrs. P. W. Penner was the spokesperson at Reedley, strongly encouraging an organization. When missionary Agnes Wiens heard of it she wrote with enthusiasm, "We want to let you know that we are very glad a committee of ladies has been formed to act as mediator between the sewing societies and the missionaries.... While we were in America I tried to stir up such an arrangement and am so very glad these sisters did not forget about it and brought up the matter at conference time."[1]

Elected to shape the new organization as Executive Committee were three women who would demonstrate remarkable qualities of leadership and foresight. Susannah Haury, Martha Goerz, and Anna Isaac had been a part of General Conference involvement for many years.

Susannah and her husband, Samuel, had been the first General Conference missionaries sent out to serve the Cheyenne and Arapaho in Indian Territory, now Oklahoma. In a day when mission boards hired the man without actually taking into account a wife's interests and abilities, Susannah contributed unique gifts. As a graduate of the Moravian Girls' Academy, she was one of the earliest Mennonite women to have an advanced education. She was an attractive and capable woman with great organizational ability. The word "efficiency" is one she used often in describing her goals for the women's organization. She graciously opened her door to many guests, and, in the custom of that day, always referred to her husband as "Doctor."

Martha Goerz was the daughter of Christian and Susannah Krehbiel. Her father was one of the early giants of the conference. She recalled that their home in Halstead, Kansas, had a steady stream of guests throughout her growing years. She and her husband, Rudolph, a Newton businessman, continued that pattern of hospitality and familiarity with civic and conference leaders, as well as close association with Bethel College faculty and students. Her term of office with the women's organization was interrupted by severe health problems, but she reentered the work with a sensitive appraisal of herself: "I am anxious to do all I can in the Lord's work and to do it to the best of my ability after he has again found fit to use me. It certainly is hard to be 'laid on the shelf.'"[2] As strength returned, she again became a vigorous and outstanding leader of the women, serving not only as secretary, but subsequently as vice-president, editor, and counselor.

Anna Isaac, a sister of India missionary P. A. Penner, had her interest in India furthered by following his progress. When a student at Bethel College, she met another student, Ferdinand Isaac, whom she would later marry, and together they would become missionaries to India. At the time she became treasurer of the women's organization, they were working in city missions in California. A tall, stately woman, Anna would go to India within two years after her election as treasurer. Years later when the missionary association published biographies of missionaries, they would write of Anna, "Time has brought Anna Isaac great joys and satisfactions, but she has known, too, the despair and spiritual impoverishment of India and the loneliness of life on an isolated mission station. Nor has God spared her 'valley of shadow' experiences."[3] Three of their four children died, one as they were coming home from India.

Anna was succeeded as treasurer by Frieda Regier (Entz) who was to serve for a full thirty years. Although not one of the original committee, Frieda Regier must be mentioned as one of those who helped shape the Women's Missionary Association. Frieda spent her early childhood on an Indian reservation in Arizona where her parents, H. R. and Barbara Voth, were missionaries, and she retained a lifelong interest in that work. Frieda's first husband, J. G. Regier, was treasurer of the Foreign Mission Board for many of the years Frieda was treasurer of the women's organization and there must have been many conversations about the financial state of the General Conference. When she retired she told the committee that the organization had come to be for her the children she never had, and giving it up was very difficult. She said, "Now that the thing is really here—I mean for me to really give up this work which has become a very part of myself—it feels a little different! . . . Ich will und will auch nicht, aber ich musz!" ("I want to and don't want to, but I must!")[4]

These four women molded the General Conference women's organization in forms which in retrospect seem truly extraordinary.

The official minutes of the 1917 conference would not have one word about the birth of a new organization, and the only public reference to it was one sentence in the editorial of the September 27, 1917, *The Mennonite* summarizing the conference. The editor wrote, "Women's work received its proper emphasis at one of the evening meetings and plans are afoot for bringing about more unity and greater effort along this line."[5]

It remained for the women themselves to announce their new involvement a half year later with the following item on the front page of the February 7, 1918, *The Mennonite* and in *Der Bote*:

At the General Conference held at Reedley, California, last fall a special business meeting of all the sewing and mission societies was called. At this meeting, a committee, consisting of three members, was chosen for the purpose of bringing the mission and sewing societies of our conference into closer touch with our foreign missionaries. This committee consists of Mrs. S. S. Haury, Upland, California, president; Mrs. R. A. Goerz, Newton, Kansas, treasurer; and Mrs. F. J. Isaac, Woodlake, California, secretary. In order to procure the greatest efficiency, the field has been divided so that Mrs. Goerz will be directly in touch with the societies of Nebraska, Kansas and Oklahoma, and Mrs. Haury with the societies of the eastern states, and Mrs. Isaac with those of the West, Northwest, and Canada. If any society anywhere should not hear from one of these three women within one month, will you kindly let us know. We need the support and assistance of every society.

When the three elected women held their first meeting in a car on a hot August afternoon, they faced each other and asked, "Where do we go from here?" There were few guidelines, no simple maps and charts to point directions for them, and at that moment of beginnings they undoubtedly felt both elation and "a trembling heart."[6] They were sure, as is evidenced in many of the letters that followed, that in working cooperatively rather than in separate units there would be more joy and greater efficiency. It was up to the three of them to devise a system which would enlarge that dream of cooperation and efficiency, and incorporate at the heart of the program a firm bond between the missionary families and the local church groups. Anna Isaac would report to the mission societies a year later, "We had but a dim vision of the possibilities and opportunities that lay before us, and the measures of procedure to make the best of these possibilities and opportunities seemed still more vague to us."[7]

The setting up of a working organization of women, eager to cooperate, is remarkable not only in the light of the creativity for which it called, but the handicaps under which they worked.

A young Canadian, writing a college term paper on the women's auxiliary forty years later, correctly analyzed the beginnings. He wrote, "One of the first groups to see the practical applications of mission work were the women in the churches. Much pushing and encouraging was necessary on the part of the executive to get the various societies to see the need of working together."[8]

There were no funds available, and for over two years the committee members bore all expenses among themselves. Finally in the third year, they asked supporting members to contribute five cents per member annually for expenses.

Travel for women was quite limited, so almost all their

decision making for many years was by correspondence. A sort of round robin was the chief means of communication, with all letters being sent to each committee member in turn for her to read and add to, which meant that it was weeks before decisions could be reached, particularly if there was much difference of opinion. It was very common for a letter to begin with apologies for delay—children were ill, or one's husband had to be readied for some trip. Perhaps the writer herself had the flu, or a relative had died, or a neighbor had to be helped out. One writer said she hadn't been able to get the letter sent because they had had forty-seven guests at their home the previous two weeks, many of whom had had at least one meal with them!

Letters from missionaries, or other business, were sent along from one committee member to the other, with many copied by hand to keep as reference. Typed letters were rare for a decade, and even later when the Literature Committee made available programs to anyone requesting them, they asked for volunteers to type the programs. In one letter Susannah fretted, "I wish we could get together and talk things over, how much more effective it would be!"[9]

One of the biggest frustrations in the beginning was the uphill road to being recognized by the conference. The initial step of the organization was to find out the names and locations of all missionary societies, as there was no complete listing anywhere. The second step was to write all missionaries asking them to tell of their needs which a women's group could supply. This was done with the permission of the Foreign Mission Board, and assignments were made on that basis within a short time.

The mission board was the most powerful arm of the General Conference, and almost everyone was familiar with the names of P. H. Richert, A. S. Shelly, M. M. Horsch, H. D. Penner, J. W. Kliewer, Gustav Harder, S. M. Musselman, W. S. Gottschall, S. F. Sprunger, H. P. Krehbiel, David Toews, and G. A. Haury. Although voluminous reports of their work and activity appeared in all church papers, there was never any mention of the women's missionary society as a supporting body. Susannah Haury pushed Rev. M. M. Horsch, a member of the board and apparently a close friend, to secure formal recognition of their organization by the board, but to no avail. Finally a letter from a Mrs. Mosiman, an "educated" woman,[10] asking Mrs. Haury with what credentials they were making assignments, brought the matter to a head. Once more Susannah went to her friend Horsch pressing for the needed recognition. Saying that Mrs. Mosiman had a perfect right to ask for credentials, she wrote to her committee:

> I spoke to Rev. Horsch again about that 'official recognition.'. . . I said that the Comm. really had no right to exist unless it was so recognized, but he was very urgent that the Comm. go on with its working, asking whether that was not official recognition enough that they turned the Girls School in China over to the women. I answered that I know the board was satisfied, but the public ought to know it. He said again that he had bro't the matter up 3 times in Board meeting, and he felt that was recognition enuf, if it had been suggested that we sit in the Board Meetings. He would not bring up the matter in a Board Meeting again, but would write the Secretary privately, not in an official capacity. So that is where the matter stands now, but I am in hopes it will be cleared up in time[11]

In less than a month the secretary of the board made public reference to the new General Conference women's organization. A startled Frieda Regier, who had succeeded Anna Isaac as treasurer, wrote to the committee:

> By the way, what do you think of the 'official recognition' given us by the Board lately in the papers? I nearly fell over, I was so surprised when I read it. Is that about what you thought they would give us? I must say that the sentence, 'Die Schwestern haben gute arbeit getan und die Behörde uberläszt ihne auch noch ferner diese Vermittlung' ("The sisters have done good work, and the board will allow them further mediation") struck me rather peculiar. I think it sounds rather weak, at least the last

part. But I may misunderstand the good man entirely. [12] Mrs. Haury doubted the board was as tentative sounding as it appeared.

Although there was now public acknowledgment of the establishment of an official women's organization, the battle for acceptance was by no means over. To help their widespread constituency keep abreast of their involvement and to promote a feeling of unity, the committee turned to the church papers, *The Mennonite* and *Der Bote*, as a medium of communication. The editor of *Der Bote*, C. H. van der Smissen, was very cooperative and published their contributions regularly, but *The Mennonite* editor, S. M. Grubb, was far less cooperative. Often he chose not to print what was submitted, and on frequent occasions he would place the information given him in scattered spots throughout the paper so there was no apparent feeling of unified effort. The women complained that it was obvious Grubb found all the space he needed for nonconference news, but there wasn't enough space to publish their conference activity.

Susannah wrote, "It seems to me the women have proven themselves worthy of a little consideration." [13] Martha Goerz was more vigorous in her disgust with the editor's scattering of their materials and her firm belief that they should have a regularly placed column when she wrote, "This may sound like Women's Rights, but I think it should be done for the good of the cause." [14]

The women felt keenly the continued pressure by some of the conference leaders to keep them from becoming too strong. Years later when the question of preserving for history the early papers and publications of the Women's Missionary Association (WMA) came up and it was suggested their materials be sent to Silas Grubb, the president wrote, "I know Silas Grubb was quite antagonistic to Woman's Work, but perhaps he's gotten over that by now. I only know he is very enthusiastic about anything and everything that may be valuable as historical material." [15]

The reason for the opposition is obscure, but perhaps

Martha put her finger on a sensitive spot when she later declared, "It is hard for some of our men to realize that women can do other things besides keeping house and raising families. Of course these things should not be neglected. But women's religious and missionary work can be systematized and strengthened so much by cooperation. I do not believe there is a woman in our conference who would willingly hinder the work of the mission board. And if they would only work with us we ought to be a mutual benefit to each other." [16]

Mennonite women were not the only ones having difficulty in being accepted, much less welcomed; it was true of both Catholic and Protestant groups as well. *Missionary News and Notes* in February 1931 carried the following reprint from the *International Journal of Religious Education* written by a Presbyterian, and one can guess the Executive Committee felt kinship and some delight as they read:

> This development of (women's) national organizations was not without opposition as one divine in an editorial gloomily observed: "Some thoughtful minds are beginning to ask, what is to become of this women's movement in the Church?" and then taking heart of grace continued, "Let them alone . . . all through our history like movements have started. Do not oppose them and it will die." His gracious hopes were not to be realized. The women continued their agitation, aided and abetted by the missionaries who knew the terrible need on the field and by the broaderminded brethren at home who had not imbibed that fear of what the women might do if left to themselves, which concerned one of the early pastors. He always attended the women's missionary meetings because, he said, "You never could tell what those women might take to praying if left alone." [17]

Members of the committee occasionally sat in on the mission board meetings at their invitation. They had sincere respect for the men they saw grappling with the problems of mission work and administration. Missionaries told them that the time had come for women to be represented on the board, but they were ahead of their time; it would be decades before that happened. For the women, love for God and the work of the church grew. They could see ways in which women's gifts could be used to carry on and promote mission endeavors, and they were determined to be participants.

A resolution passed at the 1920 triennial read: "that the conference give a vote of thanks to the Women's Mission Societies for their valuable help in the department of special gifts."[18]

At the second triennial session, following their small beginning, Martha Goerz rejoiced, "The women certainly did take part at the business meeting and the spirit of the meeting was different than ever before. Other meetings impressed me as though the people just came to listen to what the exec. com. had to say. This time it was *their* meeting and everybody took part and that is why I let them talk and talk."[19]

The organization was on firm footing. The women belonged.

Missionary "Back Up"

One of the primary reasons for organizing a missionary society conference-wide was to bring missionary and church into closer fellowship and to undergird the work of the missionary with specific help. One missionary from India expressed it, "With all the sewing societies our conference has there ought to be 1 or 2 societies for *backing up* each mission station."[20]

Before the conference organization of societies, scattered local groups worked independently. Several of these had written to missionaries whom they knew, or to stations in which they had a special interest. The missionary quoted above, for example, mentioned they had received items from Waldheim and Hillsboro. In order to relate to the asking groups, the missionaries had to write frequent letters, often duplicated, telling the societies what they needed, and describing in detail what sizes and shapes they were requesting. This necessary duplication of letters and instructions was quite time consuming, and it is easy to understand why the missionaries themselves were pleased with the organization of a central agency to which they need write only once.

The WMA Executive Committee, on the other hand, struggled several years to get the local groups to let them handle the missionary correspondence-instruction before many local groups finally permitted them to do the intermediary correspondence.

In less than a year, the "back up" for the missionaries would be termed a successful and satisfying venture. Largely through the founding committee, there was support not only for the station, but for the missionary. Each missionary family was contacted by mail for their needs for the station, and soon the term *want lists* was familiar to every mission society. Each interested group was assigned a mission station and a missionary family. Thus the work of the conference not only became personal and vital, but so did the people performing the tasks in behalf of the conference.

Missionaries were asked for the needs of the station and also for the wants of their entire family. They were frequently asked for sizes of clothing for each, as well as for anything they wanted in general. Some missionaries declined to specify, saying their wants were being met. Others sent lists in some detail. One missionary asked for a bicycle for his assistant for a Christmas gift, and a Ford for himself. "Some people are too modest, but others are free enough that is certain," was Susannah's comment. [21]

Whatever their replies, the missionary family became very personal to the supporting group, and, judging by some of the personal "want lists," the supporters also became special friends. Where the missionary might have hesitated in asking the Foreign Mission Board, he or she felt free to ask the supporting women's groups for *Alpenkreuter*, for example, or Kellogg's Corn Flakes. Requests for clothing and books were most frequent.

The birthday lists which became a feature of mission literature were a direct result of recognizing the missionary family as persons of importance, and personal correspondence was and is encouraged with members of the mission family.

The October 1926 issue of *Missionary News and Notes* had the following announcement: "During this past summer four new babies came to our missionaries in China. On Sept. 16 a little daughter to Dr. and Mrs. A. M. Lohrentz, and a son each to Rev. and Mrs. H. J. Brown, Rev. and Mrs. P. J. Boehr and Rev. and Mrs. W. C. Voth." [22] One can be sure that persons on both sides of the ocean rejoiced with that good news.

The P. J. Wiens's silver wedding anniversary was announced and celebrated, as were other occasions. Christmas gifts, both cash and material, were sent to missionary families as a matter of course. Though money amounts seem small by present-day standards, the names of those receiving this special attention read like a "Who's Who Among Missionaries."

A packer for WMA mentions putting items in tin oatmeal boxes and then to protect the packages from rough handling, she filled in all the hollow places on the sides with dried fruit of various kinds. Upon receiving one such carefully packaged item, Martha Burkhalter wrote from India, "Oh, the repeated exclamations and outbursts of astonishment when the prunes, apricots, peaches and raisins came out . . . walnuts, almonds, jelly, honey and the rest of the clothing." [23] P. A. Penner added, "Whoever has not been away from all these luxuries for years will hardly realize or fully understand the gratitude of our co-workers." [24]

One little boy growing up on an Indian reservation in Montana learned about peppernuts when a mission society sent an extra gift at Christmastime. Filling his pockets with the spicy cookies as he trudged off to school, the lad developed a fondness for their taste. Now, as an adult, David Habegger has a hobby of collecting peppernut recipes, a legacy from some thoughtful mission group. [25]

When a baby or a child died, and there were many, the missionary parents were surrounded by prayers and concern, although the belated communications meant that knowledge could not be shared for several weeks.

Concern for the missionary family was not limited to gestures overseas. The children of missionaries sent to school in the United States or Canada received special attention and were frequently asked to share about their lives in an overseas setting. Families often provided a home away from home for them and tried to substitute for some of the care their parents could not give them. At one meeting at Bluffton College, the speaker noted,

> I often wonder if we appreciate having so many missionary children in our midst. Most of us are mothers, and those of us who are and have our children far from home, know how it warms our hearts when some one has been to see our children and then comes and tells us about that visit, tells us something good about them. We love to hear it. Our missionary parents are just like we are. Many a missionary child has taken part in our programs. We could have written to their parents and told them how well their son or daughter did. Some did do that very thing and gladdened the hearts of lonely parents. But I wonder how many did. [26]

Children on this continent were encouraged to write "mish kids" on other continents, and friendships developed as letters were shared in church and school. Missionary families held a unique position in the church, due in part to the warm publicity given them by women's missionary societies.

All this esteem for missionaries had its drawbacks also. Because the missionary was held in such high regard, there seems to have been little question in the minds of many that the missionary was the ultimate authority and all requests should be automatically granted. Those of their number who

14

spoke and wrote more fluently, who were outgoing and good in public relations, carried more weight than did the less vocal person who went about his or her business quietly, although their suggestions were just as legitimate. Uneven giving sometimes resulted.

On their part missionaries quickly recognized that the response from the women's organization was frequently more favorable and more quickly offered than that of the Foreign Mission Board. So they began to bypass the board in favor of the women's groups, both local and General Conference, although they had been told repeatedly that they were not to contact local groups directly. The committee balked when one missionary wrote to the organization saying that what they really needed was houses for their workers. A policy was established in which they declared they would not pay for buildings unless they were in the Foreign Mission Board's budget, and then they would be contributing partners only.

Sometimes when there was disagreement among the missionaries on a given field, the women found themselves caught in the middle. One time after they had sent their annual requests for "want lists," a missionary working with American Indians wrote them that the missionaries had agreed among themselves that the time for material-aid handouts to the Indians was over, that the Indians were not helpless and were quite capable of taking care of their own needs, and, therefore, that aspect of the mission program should be discontinued. A few days later the committee received a letter from a missionary on the same field a few miles away with a long list of things to be sent to the station. What were they to do? Letters went back and forth among the Executive Committee members, and in the end they decided that, since they had asked for the lists, they were under obligation to answer in the manner requested. They refused to take sides and would let the missionaries iron out their problems in their own way. Missionaries, independent by necessity, were not always easy to work with, and the women's goal to correlate giving was not a simple matter to carry out.

Station "Back Up"

"Back up" for the mission station meant something else. Budgets for stations were carefully planned by the Foreign Mission Board and usually devoid of extras. For many years the support of women's groups was called *special gifts* by the board, as contrasted with budget giving. The term was a misnomer. Why paying for plumbing, electricity, school supplies, digging wells, travel, and countless other necessities constituted gifts instead of budget is not easy to understand.

Even before there was an official Women's Missionary Association there were local groups lending strong support. Wadsworth Seminary, the official institution of higher learning for the General Conference, opened its doors in 1868, with dormitory bedding and linens furnished by women's societies. The first General Conference mission group at Donnellson, Iowa, was organized in part to enable the women to work together at providing those needed linens. A group at Bally, Pennsylvania, which was the second to be organized, contributed its share for Wadsworth in the early years, as did other groups in that area.

Mission work with Arapaho and Cheyenne in Indian Territory (Oklahoma) was the first "foreign" mission work of the conference. When the Hopi Indians in Arizona and the Cheyenne in Montana were included later, that was also known as "foreign" until taken over by the Commission on Home Ministries in 1969. The term was used because the missionary had to learn a language other than the Mennonite's English or German.

When Samuel Haury, a member of the first Wadsworth graduating class, and Susannah went to Indian territory to become the first General Conference missionaries, women at Halstead, Kansas, organized in their support. The Haurys were especially concerned about education as one of the most

16

urgent needs of Indians, and so immediately built a boarding school. Halstead women furnished bedding, towels, and tea towels. A tragic fire a short time later burned the boarding school to the ground, taking the lives of two Indian boys, the Haury's son, Carl Albert, and their adopted Indian daughter, Jennie.[27] The Halstead women were instant in their help once again to reequip a new school which was built. Their records also show that they canned peaches and made jellies and pickles for the new school, probably because they were near enough to transport these items without too much difficulty.

When work opened among the Cheyenne in Montana and the Hopi in Arizona, this also became a part of the material-aid program of the societies. By the time the women were organized in 1917 there were sixty-seven societies, all of them involved in some way with the mission program.

Sewing was a part of the initial contact between the women's organization and missions in America. Baby clothing, dresses, aprons, shirts, and overalls were made, although the women complained about handling heavy overall material. Christmas lists made out by the missionaries included requests for clothing, cash for Christmas treats, dolls and other toys, books, Bibles, and school supplies.

Though well intentioned, the sewing could be considered only partly successful. Understandably, dresses which were sewed to fit no one in particular fit no one in particular, and sometimes the choice of colors and patterns did not appeal to Indian tastes. Several missionaries asked that no sewing be sent, but that they be given cash for materials for people to do their own sewing or to buy clothing from Sears, Roebuck & Co. which would fit. Mrs. Rudolphe Petter was one who asked that there be no further sewing, saying, "Our women can make beautiful comforts, and one is before me as I write, which I would like to send to some of our ladies in the churches. Mr. Habegger drolly remarked, 'If you do, no one will want to make a comfort for the Indians again.'"[28] Eventually quilt blocks, yardage, and sewing supplies replaced the finished items, but it was a lesson learned slowly.

In India the tiny new congregations called *mission compound congregations* by Jim Juhnke in his book *A People of Mission* were made up of poor people. Juhnke writes,

> When the Mennonite mission celebrated its twenty-fifth anniversary there were only 115 Christian families in the four mission station churches at Champa, Janjgir, Korba, and Mauhadih. Of this group, 85 percent depended upon the mission for salaries or support. Less than a quarter of the members owned their own houses, land, or cattle. It was a poor church, drawn from the outcastes, separated onto the mission station, and dependent in the long run upon mission institutions financed from North America. [29]

It was for these people that the "want lists" were made out in the early years of the women's societies, and the mission circles became veritable factories in the production of goods. American women became familiar with *cholies* and *dhotis* and *leper jackets*.

To read the reports is to realize there must have been hundreds, and perhaps thousands, of Indian boys and girls running around in pants identically made according to the following directions:

Boys and Girls Pants for India

They should be knee length and closed both back and front. Cut front and back exactly alike—legs not too wide at knee. Sew up all seams—leave no opening. Then put a wide hem or casing around the top through which you draw a drawstring made of the material or a strong tape. The ends of the drawstring come out to tie through two buttonholes near the front seam or through an opening made by folding down the hem. Be sure and tack the drawstring at the back so it does not pull out.

For the boys use heavy shirting, gingham or still better khaki or lightweight overall goods. For the smaller girls use blue or gray gingham and for the larger unbleached muslin. [30]

Who would care to guess how many sizes of garments resulted when made from instructions to make "armhole normal size, not too large and not too tight for the size of the waist?"[31]

To carry out the sending of these garments, bedding, and food, sewing supervisors were chosen in each district to make assignments and to divide the work evenly. The items were then sent to packers chosen by the organization at Berne, Indiana, and Reedley, California. Theirs was a hard, demanding task as they had to supply the crates and pack them carefully.

The triennial reports from 1923-1926 show that thousands of items were sent as follows:

1923-1926	India	China	Montana	Arizona	City Missions	Others
Children's clothing	2,546	24	1,945	61	272	201
Girls' clothing	4,904	7	1,241	41	149	187
Women's clothing	2,936	54	1,664	74	68	204
Boys' clothing	2,976	20	737	40	53	50
Men's clothing	1,572	83	1,608	70	45	81
Bedding	449	19	731	82	40	154
Jackets for lepers	1,119	-	-	-	-	-

By the 1935 triennium the amounts were considerably smaller, as shown below:

1933-1936	India	Montana	Arizona	City Missions	Other
Clothing	720	1,508	1,492	48	540
Used clothing	20	24	-	815	1,650 lbs.
Bedding	125	210	124	14	65

From 1917 to 1934, 54,560 pounds of materials were sent to India alone.[32]

Missionaries in India sought to promote their field by assigning the names of needy widows and orphans, and the records of the women's organization are filled with accounts of money given to specific people. It is obvious that there was no way this could be carried out practically, but it served one important purpose; it helped to personalize the work of

19

missions and it brought a tremendous response from those who found helping people more satisfying than helping program. When the method was discontinued and sewing assignments decreased, so did contributions, and a number of societies disbanded.

The editor of *Missionary News and Notes* questioned why sewing was such an essential. "Why do we women find it so much easier to buy material and send a garment than to give the money? Does the gift look bigger to us if it is sewed?"[33] There was no satisfactory answer.

Four years later the president of the WMA was still struggling with the importance of sewing, "This shows the need of something to take the place of sewing. . . . I'm afraid unless the women have something definite to meet for they may simply leave it to their husbands to do the giving and lose interest."[34] Sewing assignments in decreasing numbers continued until the late thirties. In the forties, membership in the Congo Inland Mission Auxiliary brought about another type of material aid, which will be discussed in another chapter.

It is interesting to note that sewing for China never reached the proportions shown for India. This was due in no small part to the missionaries who kept advising the Executive Committee that it was neither reasonable nor economical to send sewed garments to China. As early as March 31, 1919, Jennie Boehr wrote: "We however wish to say once more that we really think it (sewing garments) an unwise plan. If the ladies wish to see the biggest returns for their efforts it is really a waste of money and time on their part as we here on the field look at it."[35] She went on to prove her point by showing that a gold dollar in the United States bought five yards of calico, but the same amount of money in China would buy forty feet of material in preferable color and design. Later they asked for money to buy sewing materials, which was given.

The first large project for China, therefore, was the building of a girls' school at the cost of $5,000. The Foreign

Mission Board advanced the money so that building could begin immediately, but before the women had raised the full amount, the school was closed down. However, they continued their fund drive until they reimbursed the amount they had pledged.

By 1939 the sewing supervisors were renamed *district advisers*, as the sewing decreased and their duties changed accordingly. They acted as liaisons between the districts and the General Conference, interpreting the activities and goals of each to the other conference, and were a valuable asset to the organization. Responsibilities increased with the change, and they were asked to attend the annual business planning meetings of the missionary association. Although not given voting privileges in the council until 1971,[36] in actual practice they were a working part of that body, and their opinions were solicited and appreciated.

It was in 1952, thirty-five years after the organization began, that "want lists" disappeared from the mission scene. The WMA minutes record: "It was agreed that we ask the general secretary of the mission board to inform the missionaries on all fields that the WMA is discontinuing its request letter for want lists, so all requests of missionaries should be included in their budget askings to the mission board."[37]

Taiwan was an area of mission work to which material aid was given after "want lists" were discontinued. The Mennonite Central Committee (MCC) had begun medical relief work in 1950 at the invitation of the Presbyterian workers who were concerned about the medical needs of the mountain people. MCC instituted a mobile medical clinic, which it turned over to the General Conference in 1954. The term *Taiwan Aid* first appeared in the district advisers' assignment sheets ten years later. At that time, assignments for the Children's Home and the Mennonite Christian Hospital were made through MCC. They included sewing for infants, boys, and girls, and providing certain hospital linens. Cash assignments which were also forwarded by MCC were included as well. By 1978 all giving to Taiwan was in cash.

Only a few items, sewed for Zaire in that year, were all that remained of the program that began with thousands of garments. Still needed was the backup of intelligent support, prayer, money, and concern.

2 missions nearer home

When the societies organized at the triennial conference in 1917, the Mennonite woman eagerly joined the ranks of those concerned about "the great cause of missions."[1] Her awareness of herself as a contributor to home missions was less conscious. Of course, one helped one's neighbor, but there was nothing special about that. You shared food with the hungry, left your home to wait on those who were sick, and sent your children to help out where physical assistance was needed. You gave bedding and simple household furnishings to those who needed them, and you always had room and food for one more guest in your home. You comforted the dying and bereaved with your warm presence, and a dish of food for the gathering of relatives and friends. That was just being neighborly.

Before the first decade of its existence was over, the WMA was being nudged by current events to become active in missions near home. The migration of Mennonites to Canada in the twenties, thirties, and forties brought many people who needed help not only for employment and housing but even for survival in some cases. They were helped first and most often by Canadians themselves, but more help was needed as over twenty thousand people entered Canada between 1923 and 1930. [2]

Early records show that contributions of food and clothing were sent by women's societies in the United States. One entry is a "donation for Hospital care for immigrants who might be deported." [3] There are frequent entries simply labeled "Freight for Canada," and some groups gave directly through their churches. "Harbin refugees" were designated as recipients, but the record is incomplete. [4]

A concerned Canadian sent an appeal which was published in the December 1926 *Missionary News and Notes*: "Mrs. H. H. Ewert, Gretna, Manitoba, has written to several societies about the condition of 15 families of the Russian immigrants who are studying in the academy at Gretna. She asks for contributions in money to help buy a sack of flour for each family for Christmas."

Immigrant girls went to Canada's large cities to seek work to support themselves and provide money which had been advanced for their families' passports. In December 1925 David Toews of Rosthern wrote to the conference asking for help in providing a place for the girls to stay, fearing they would be lost in the cities. Over five hundred girls would stay in homes in Winnipeg, Saskatoon, and Vancouver. [5] The Women's Missionary Association provided some of the funds. Helen Peters, who served as housemother for girls in a home in Winnipeg, wrote in 1927, "Our main work of course is with our many girls who come to Winnipeg to work as housemaids. . . . Our work is really very taxing. Especially, because the means and possibilities at our disposal as house, furnishings and workers are so limited. . . . Especially do we want to direct this writing to the Women's Societies. . . . 'Our girls!' What isn't involved in those words!" [6]

Two women who never met felt love for each other as the Canadian recipient of a gift shared, "Our baby received a pair of pale blue stockings with a slip attached to it saying, 'Pleasant growth for the little pilgrim, is the wish of A

Grandmother.' How we would like to go to that grandmother in Kansas and thank her personally."[7]

Then came the depression years, and financial problems increased. The hard times in late 1929 meant a loss of jobs for thousands, and bread lines became common. Unemployment reached 25 percent of the United States population and some estimates ran higher. *Relief* was a word used for people at home as well as for immigrants and persons overseas. Added to this were drought, dust storms, and crop failures through the midsection of the United States and Canada. Both Mennonite and non-Mennonite farmers lost everything when they couldn't make payments on their heavily mortgaged farms. Small businesses folded. Many women recall when flour sacks and mash sacks were carefully used as precious yardage. It was a time not only of depression of finances but depression of spirit.

The mission board found itself unable to meet budgets. Frieda Regier notified the committee, "The Mission Bd. cut salaries and budgets 10% and now it seems they will have to cut some more."[8] *Missionary News and Notes* reported in December 1935, "Due to an unusual amount of illness among the missionaries in India during the past few months some families ought to come home on furlough, but the Foreign Mission Board cannot grant these requests or send out badly needed new missionaries until sufficient funds are available for this purpose."[9]

The fiftieth anniversary year for General Conference missions was 1930, commemorating the opening of work with Indians; and the mission board made a great effort to show real celebration for that historic commitment by asking all persons to help wipe out the conference debt. Mennonites reached deep into their limited resources and erased the debt, but after that effort there was again a slump in giving. The 1932 triennial sessions were postponed to save on travel costs, and during the following triennium the Executive Committee of the women's association met only by mail.

When the conference was held in 1933, the WMA passed the following resolution: "That we thank our Heavenly Father that even through this depression our books still show a credit rather than a debit and we recommend that we speak of the many blessings rather than the depression."[10]

Once more David Toews wrote to the conference, apologizing for having to ask for help again.

I had really hoped that it would not be necessary this year, but drouth, grasshoppers, rust and in some places hail have damaged our crops to a very great degree.... I would like to remind you that in large areas in Canada we have not had crops for the last six or seven years, and I would ask you to further consider that we have had thousands of families of people who came over to us from Russia stripped of all their belongings.[11]

A pamphlet entitled *Home Missions* published by the WMA Literature Committee provided an interesting account by Toews of the Canadian immigration years.

Sewing for India had decreased, and the years of tight money were natural ones to slow down the program further. Adah B. Wenger discreetly advised,

We sincerely wish that our sisters at home, who have given their time so nobly to the sewing work, may not misunderstand. We are not unappreciative of your help and do not wish to cut off your avenues of help. We hope it may mean to you not a ceasing of activity but working in a different line. I have been thinking hard as to what we might suggest for those to do who prefer to work with their hands to promote the cause here. This seems difficult to suggest, since this would no doubt depend a great deal upon the various committees. But we here at Basna are convinced that if somehow that work could be turned into money at home and the money be sent to us, the value realized here would be doubled or tripled. May I give you a concrete illustration. Recently one society sent us fifteen dollars instead of sixteen shirts which had been alloted to them to sew for our station, stating that we are sending fifteen dollars to buy sixteen shirts. By actual experience I know that I can provide at least sixty shirts of good strong durable cloth for that sum of money. Another society sent twenty-five dollars for the same purpose. If the hard cash which had been put into the purchasing of clothing in America and the sending of the same to India were sent to us in money it would not only provide much more clothing, but would help to provide the means by which the children here could be taught to do their own sewing.[12]

With the decrease in sewing it was no longer necessary to have two packers to send materials to India, and all shipping was done after this time from Berne, Indiana.

Civilian Public Service

While Mennonites continued to struggle with shortages of funds and what that was doing to our mission program, Hitler began to move Germany to take over western Europe. Canadian and American people looked on, as it were, from a distance, thinking it was someone else's problem more than theirs. However, when England declared war on Germany on September 3, 1939, Canada followed with a declaration of war one week later. The United States entered officially with the Japanese bombing of Pearl Harbor on December 7, 1940. Once again Mennonites had to face the issue of war and pacifism, but this time they were better prepared than they had been for World War I. For Mennonite families, Civilian Public Service (CPS) would become a factor of much significance, and the Women's Missionary Association would become active helpers in the peace witness.

The first two CPS camps were ready in April 1941. In February of that year representatives of the WMA had met with Dr. H. A. Fast, director of the CPS program, to see how they could make their contributions for the camps. It was decided that instructions would appear in *Missionary News and Notes* to keep members current with the program and to assist them in preparing the necessary donations. In some areas, the WMA would be in charge of the program, working with the district peace committee, and in others, as in

Northern District, the peace committee would provide the contacts with the help of the women's groups.

The preparation of camp packs began. They included three bed sheets, two pillowcases, three hand towels, two bath towels, two washcloths, shaving supplies, dental supplies, toilet soap, hand mirror, shoe polishing supplies, stationery and stamps, emergency sewing kit, and other personal items as desired. Most of the packs were supplied by the family or the local churches of the boys in camp, but the WMA was very careful to point out that their additions were not to be construed as relief for the recipient. In *Missionary News and Notes* they wrote, "Such a pack, if presented, should be entirely with the thought of expressing in part our interest, our Christian concern, our support in the stand the young man takes for conscience' sake. In no case should it be intimated that it is offered on account of possible lack of funds on his part, or that of his parents, to purchase the articles contained therein."[13]

The WMA secretary had written each camp to offer the women's services as needs arose, and camp directors were quick to respond. Camp packs for some non-Mennonite boys were asked for, as well as for some Japanese, and for boys who were in camp against their parents' wishes. Curtains for the infirmary, dining halls, and bathrooms were called for, and sometimes for the dormitories as well. Caps for the camp cooks and waiters and long aprons for the meat cutter were among the requests, as were curtains to cover the front of wardrobes without doors. Tea towels and dishclothes, counterpanes, throw rugs, and bedding to replace torn or worn bedding were called for.

Canned and dried fruits for the camp represented another area of help in which women were the prime promoters. Sugar was rationed during the war years, and *Missionary News and Notes* advised women that they could obtain sugar ration coupons from Mennonite Central Committee for camp canning. At a meeting of the Executive Committee on June 18, 1943, it was "decided on the basis of the total number of women in our constituency we suggest that each family try to can 8 qts. or 4½-gal. jars of foodstuffs and dry as much as possible for this canning project for C.P.S. camps."[14] The women had been told by John Snyder of MCC that they would be furnished with large-size jars. The filled half-gallon jars were heavy and difficult to ship, and the WMA executives began to receive mail asking if anyone was paying shipping costs of the program. The secretary informed them, "Sooner or later it all comes from our Mennonite sources anyway, so we just help M.C.C. that much if we pay it at the start."[15]

Church and mission society worked together. From Henderson, Nebraska, came the report that one family had donated 190 quarts. The Pacific and Eastern Districts sent huge supplies of dried fruit. The Northern District WMA adviser estimated that four thousand jars had been canned in the Mt. Lake, Minnesota, community. One Kansas group wrote to WMA that it would not be possible to can in their community because of a bad gardening year, but they would like to donate chickens, eggs, potatoes, and cash for canning. Their offer was gladly accepted, but they were told they would have to see that the produce was delivered to the nearest camp by themselves. MCC assessed the value of the food at fifteen to twenty-seven cents a quart for canned fruit, ten to thirty cents a quart for canned vegetables, twelve to twenty-one cents a pound for dried fruits, and canned chicken at forty cents a quart.

The canning continued for several months after the war ended until the boys were all discharged from camps, and a new request at that time was for work clothes for returning CPSers. When it was finally over, the WMA Executive Committee reported, "C.P.S. projects, concluded in 1945, had been a wonderful means of bringing not only mothers, wives, and sisters into fellowship with the boys who gave their testimony this way, but it brought to women of the constituency in general a feeling of responsibility to thus witness to the way of Christian love in action."[16]

Migrant Work

Migrants? Are there still Migrants? This year the Federal Government estimated that 4,000,000 seasonal workers would be required to harvest and process the crops for the food supply at home and overseas. Much the larger group are native migrants: Negro, Spanish, Japanese, White Americans. The smaller groups are imported migrants from Jamaica, the Bahamas, the Barbados, and Mexico. These imported migrants, however, are to be returned now that the war is over. The native migrant is not protected by governmental agreement and as a result has had to live in many cases outside the government camps which were available to imported migrants. The problems of schooling for their children, undesirable working conditions, unfair recruiting practices, lack of medical care, religious ministry and cultural opportunity, as well as discrimination by local communities—all these still cause distressing limitations and hardship on the lives of a great group of our citizens. . . . We are grateful to say that three workers have volunteered to do migrant and mission work this summer [17]

When *Missionary News and Notes* published the above information in February 1947, the work with migrants was successfully established, and the WMA felt good about their new involvement; but their entry into migrant missions was filled with challenge and uncertainty. Just before the General Conference met in Souderton in 1941, interested women of the women's associations of the General Conference, Central Conference, and Defenseless Mennonites were asked to meet in Goshen because a need had been felt for a closer working together of the women of the missionary societies of these Mennonite groups. A little Christmas card from a sister in one branch to a sister in another branch had suggested the idea of migrant or other missionary work in the homeland. [18]

At this meeting plans were made to investigate work among migrants as a possibility of united service, with the understanding that in following years it might be another type of mission work. One woman from each conference was chosen to be on the Executive Committee for what would be known as United Mennonite Women's Service Committee (MWS). Later the word *United* was dropped from the name. The motion to enter migrant work was adopted at the triennial session, and Emma Ruth of Reedley, California, was elected to be on the committee of which she would become secretary.

The first year's work for the committee was one of exploration and learning. When they met a year later they asked each conference to bring additional women so that there would be a greater representation of the mission societies to help in decision making. At first this representation consisted of the presidents of the three groups, and later this was increased to a board, which included one representative from each of the conference districts. One of the plans they agreed upon was that the financial responsibility was to be shared on a membership basis with the General Conference and its twenty-two thousand members to carry 0.7 of the budget, Central Conference with two thousand members to pay 0.2, and Defenseless Mennonites with one thousand members, 0.1. None of the three denominations represented carried on migrant work, so it was apparent the women would have to seek other groups to work with, since they had neither the money nor the know-how to carry on such a program by themselves. Of great concern to them was that the group with which they would work must be fundamentally in harmony with the religious beliefs of the cooperating bodies.

Three possibilities the MWS investigated were the Mennonite Central Committee, the American Friends Service Committee, and the Home Mission Council. MCC informed them that they had no migrant work, nor were they planning to enter the field because of their heavy responsibilities in rehabilitation for CPS men, and needs for relief overseas following the war. (At least one member of the WMA was not too fond of working under Mennonite Central Committee.

She said, "It is also pointed out that this Com. (Mennonite Service) was given the task of arranging some work that we Menn. *Women* could work together on whereas under MCC it would be men.")[19]

Their choice was the Home Missions Council (HMC), a New York-based mission program. In 1908 twenty church boards had joined to form the council, with women's groups coming in 1911. Their first involvements included the publishing of study books and establishing the World Day of Prayer. By 1920 they had begun work among the Indians; and in 1921 work with children of migrants. On December 14, 1940, forty-two men's boards and twenty-three women's national boards united to form the Home Mission Council of North America. This was the group with which the Mennonite women would work, although they were never to join as official members of that body.

It took considerable courage and aggressiveness for the women to launch out without the overseeing and protection of the mission board, but they were propelled by two strong motives, the appeal of working as an inter-Mennonite group of women, and their concern for the migrants. Nevertheless, the Executive Committee was divided throughout the entire project on whether their decision was right. The majority felt there was much to be gained by such cooperation and that they should move ahead confidently, but a minority was not convinced, although they went along with the decisions. Their objection was never to migrant work, but some of them preferred a more evangelistic organization to work with. On two different occasions, the WMA sent a representative to attend the Home Missions Council meetings and report back to the group their impressions of what the council was like. Missionary Wilhelmena Kuyf, WMA president Marie Lohrentz, and MWS committee member Mrs. Jerry Sauder of the Defenseless Mennonites brought back solid endorsement of the council work, although they felt no need to justify all their endeavors. The first to go as observer was Wilhelmena Kuyf. Her report was very positive. She felt the work was definitely Christian, rather like a daily vacation Bible school, but naturally fuller, since the children were kept all day long and other age groups were included. She thought the evangelistic emphasis was real, and that there were unlimited opportunities in the program. [20]

To those who feared working with non-General-Conference people, Marie Lohrentz wrote,

> The reason back of the United Service Com. is a feeling that Mennonite women need to and want to find some project on which we can and will want to work together. For the purpose of *working together* and *closer fellowship* and *better understanding* among women of the various branches of Mennonites this com. came into being. We just can't without much ado throw it overboard and we go our own way and let them go theirs. The members of MCC tell us that very often they don't agree on things either at the outset of a new project, but after thinking it over, praying about it and each one giving in here or there, often just tabling it for quite a time - they find that they see the green light to move forward, and you know they haven't made any great blunders yet! [21]

After she had attended a session of the Home Missions Council, she was decidedly enthusiastic about continuing, and had no qualms about the spiritual dedication of HMC.

Mary Burkhart of the Central Conference came to the same conclusion. "I think I have learned through the investigation and Mrs. Sauder's reaction to the meeting that I feel it is allright to work with the Council. We may not always agree but Mennonites don't even among themselves and can't work together as they should. I think we Protestants must begin to work together more if we want to get things done." [22]

Emma Ruth, WMA's committee representative, suggested that perhaps the work would solicit greater response and more interest from the women if a Mennonite were employed for their migrant work, and the Executive Committee agreed fully. The Home Missions Council also expressed approval, and the search began. The committee planned to support a worker for the summer months in 1943, but, although sufficient funds had been raised by summer, they didn't find a suitable candidate; so their entry into the work was delayed until 1944 when Leonore Friesen became their first migrant worker. Leonore's description of the migrant child was convincing proof of the needs of the work.

> Many children work in the field all day long even many six-year-olds. Just yesterday I met a six year old girl whose father had gone to Arkansas to get her mother, little new baby sister and her other brothers and sister also younger than herself. He had left her here to work. She was to pick two carriers a day which would make $1.66 a day. She is but an example of many who are having no real childhood at all. [23]

The WMA had not gone into this work without consulting the General Conference Home Missions Board, which seems to have given them permission and little else. In February 1947 the mission board passed the following resolution: "Resolved that we as a board of missions approve the Women's Missionary Organization's cooperation with the Home Missions Council in the field of Migrant work. The understanding being that the Women's Missionary Organization be permitted to engage their own workers." [24] That was three years after the first worker had been employed by the women.

Marie Lohrentz suggested that A. J. Neuenschwander, secretary of the Home Missions Board, be invited to attend their inter-Mennonite committee meetings. "I would be in favor to have Rev. A. J. N. sit in and see whether this work can't be done under our Home Missions Com. I feel that might help solve our problems." [25] It was also suggested that it would be worth his while to attend Home Missions Council session, but there is no record in their minutes to indicate that he did either.

WMA's committeewoman, Emma Ruth, found the involvement very worthwhile, and she felt there were definite advantages to interdenominational experiences. She wrote,

> So perhaps we are to pioneer in participating in this interdenominational missionary work. No one can deny that the need is great, and the visible results are few because of the nature of the work. Should that keep us from offering our workers for it and giving our means? While it gives us a feeling of satisfaction to point to a certain place and group of Christian people and say, 'That is what we have done,' there is also a blessing in knowing that we can cooperate with the larger body of Christians in the HMC in grappling with problems on a large scale. [26]

By the summer of 1951, MCC began a voluntary service program with migrants, also under loose association with the Home Missions Council. By this time the General Conference Home Missions Board, prodded by the Alexanderwohl Church in Kansas which had one of its members living in Arizona who wanted to work with migrants, made a small beginning at Eloy, Arizona. Checks coming into the General Conference offices earmarked "migrant work" had been given to the WMA as the only sponsoring group, but now there was confusion about who should be given the money. The WMA secretary wrote to the Home Missions Board asking for some clarification of policy. Neuenschwander thanked them for their letter and said he was about to write an article for the church papers announcing the opening of their field and asking people to write checks for Arizona Migrant Work. Then he added: "Another way of clearing up the situation would be if either your committee or our Home Mission Section would take up both phases of the work. You could still advocate the giving of gifts for the migrant work through your channel or we direct it to you to your treasury. I would be glad to have your reaction as to what your committee feels would be the best for the whole cause." [27]

The offer seemed to suggest a logical arrangement, but

evidently the women saw it as trying to yoke system with nonsystem. The WMA secretary wrote:

> The work of the Home Mission Board was undertaken, from all appearances, without due investigation and from inadequate motivation. It is still in a very rudimentary stage. . . . I do not see how this end could be served by withdrawal from the Home Missions Council at this time, and by leaving the work to the Home Mission Board, whose major interests and concerns are still in other areas of work. We do well not to underestimate the background and overall planning of the Home Missions Council for our work, as well as the preliminary coaching of our workers as they set out. [28]

Nor, apparently, did they wish to take on the responsibility for the "rudimentary" work in Arizona.

However, in 1951 the Evangelical Conference women (formerly Defenseless) expressed their desire to work through the Mennonite Central Committee, and they withdrew from the women's alliance. Since the Central Conference had affiliated with the General Conference in 1945, there were now only the districts of General Conference women left. They continued to employ their missionaries and underwrite the full cost themselves until at the triennial sessions in 1953 they officially dissolved the program with the passing of two recommendations: (a) We recommend that the Women's Missionary Association channel its migrant work through the MCC (Board of Christian Service), giving financial support for at least two full-time workers and continue to solicit personnel for such work, these to be processed through MCC; (b) We recommend that we increase our financial support of the Mission Board at Eloy, Arizona, in order that a more effective, permanent program might be undertaken.

During this time the women had placed workers in migrant camps in New York, Michigan, Minnesota, Illinois, and Arkansas.

The twelve-year program was unique in their history.

Mountain Work

Another area of missions at home in which WMA became involved was mountain work in Cumberland, Kentucky, and Paint Rock, North Carolina. The General Conference had no mission there, but the work drew the interest of Mennonites. Elsa Grantland was one worker who had been given partial support by the Home Missions Board, and Margaret Slotter and Elsie Pfister of Lansdale, Pennsylvania, "good Mennonite girls," [29] became part of the Scripture Memory Mountain Mission. Individual societies in the Central District and Eastern District who knew the women personally contributed financially to their work, drawing the Home Missions Board into partial support for all three.

When the women's societies asked if there was something particular in the way of a project, the mission board recommended that they buy an automobile for Elsa; it was getting very hard to find parts for her fourteen-year-old Chevrolet coupe, and without a car she couldn't function effectively in the hills. After some hesitation, the WMA decided to raise money for a car, but they wanted it understood that after they bought the car someone else was responsible for its upkeep. The women promoted the project diligently until they had enough money to buy a car, only to learn that Miss Grantland had left the field, turning the work over to someone else. The Home Missions Board had neglected to inform them.

It had been the practice of the women's societies at the triennial sessions to introduce all the missionaries in the audience at their programs, frequently having all of them on the platform throughout the program. Before the 1947 conference, the Home Missions Board had written the WMA to ask that there be a more "proportionate" [30] number of home missionaries on their program, not only overseas missionaries. Just whose fault it had been that no more home missionaries had been presented is not clear from the correspondence, but the WMA was in agreement that there should be more. In addition, the WMA wrote the board

37

offering to have a home missions display at the next conference, explaining that they had always featured foreign missions displays but interest was growing for home missions, especially in mountain work. The mission board wrote them, ". . . since it is, after all, under our Board, it might be confusing if some of the exhibits were under our Board and some of our work was under your direction." [31] The offer of help was rejected. It is not surprising that the next decade found the promotion of home-mission work by the women's association at low key.

In many ways the 1940s and early 1950s were a golden era for the women's association. Between 55 to 57 percent of all women and girls between the ages of twelve and sixty-five in the congregations belonged to societies, with membership in some small churches at 100 percent. Members had both money and desire to invest. The secretary wrote, "The women, just like the public in general, have more money now than sometimes in the past and they wish to know of worthy causes and projects into which they can put it." [32]

A further strengthening factor was the vigorous effort by the executive to assure that all mission societies were made to feel they were part of the whole. In 1946/47 "practically all" [33] the mission societies in the United States and Canada were visited by a member of the Executive Committee or someone they appointed as representative. President Marie Lohrentz, who had a clergy pass on the railroad, traveled for two months to cover the most miles, and the committee divided the rest of the groups among them. Every written report mentions the questions and answers which were part of each visit. It was a pronounced learning experience for both the officers and the societies. The result was affirmation of each other; although they recognized the imperfections which existed, and a renewed understanding that an organization, after all, is persons.

Acquiring an employee, an assistant, and an office of their own meant the work no longer depended on part-time hours and personal equipment. Few were able or willing to give forty hours a week, as had secretary Matilda Voth.[34] The services of Eleanor Camp, first office secretary, and her successor, Dorothea Dyck, were to provide continuity and stability for twenty-six years.

Coupled with strong aggressive leadership, women were led into new awareness of their potential. If they were still interested in a "Frauenecke," ("women's corner"), it was a much bigger corner than the founders had envisioned.

3 promotion through print

One of the most valuable, though underrated, aspects of the women's missionary organization was its emphasis on the need to inform the congregation. If any kind of mission effort was to continue, the supporting body would have to be knowledgeable. The women firmly believed that you learned more if you had information at hand to which you could refer.

An overview of their publications by decades provides a profile of women's interests. Their first publication in the twenties began:

> One day (about two years ago) a man named Garib, of the grass-cutter caste, came to my bungalow and asked if I had any work for him to do. He was poor and had a family of four children to support. After a short conversation he expressed his desire of becoming a Christian. [1]

In the 1930s their great concern was with the missionaries in China who were caught in the Sino-Japanese conflict. *Missionary News and Notes* published a letter from three missionary mothers:

Kikungshan, Honan, China, Sept. 12, 1937
Here on the mountain we have been much disturbed lately

owing to the many letters from the American Embassy urging Americans to withdraw from China as soon as possible. . . . At the present we, mothers and children, are continuing to live in Kikungshan, because the consul very emphatically says we should not return into the interior. We are especially affected because our field is in the danger zone. Also the School Board passed a decision that children belonging to non-cooperating missions must have at least one parent here, so that in case of possible evacuation they will be here to take care of their own children. Richard Pannabecker and Stanley Voth are both in high school so we feel it important to keep them here, the other children we have placed in school also to give them the advantage of mingling with other children. . . . Some missionaries have evacuated to Hong Kong, others to Manila. . . . Many feel that if everyone were to go home now, it would be most difficult to open up work again in the future. . . . An air raid was expected last night on a nearby aerodrome, so we had to extinguish all lights.

Sincerely yours,
Mrs. S. F. Pannabecker
Mrs. W. C. Voth
Mrs. C. L. Pannabecker [2]

Publications in the forties dealt with internment of church workers during World War II. Wilhelmena Kuyf, long familiar to the women's mission organization, told them in *Internment Echoes*,

The growing tensions during the fall of 1941 in occupied China had prepared us for what was to come, so that when we three Mennonites and five Nazarenes were interned in December 8 it was no great surprise. Not one of us knew what was in store. Our devotions the first evening brought out repeatedly the thought that in God was our sure defense. We prayed that we might give an effective witness when we were questioned. The first two weeks of our internment brought frequent visits from the Japanese military and always the questions, "Why are you here?" "How long have you been in China?" They seemed much impressed by Rev. and Mrs. Brown's record of thirty-two years. . . . How full of meaning Paul's writings became! [3]

The forties also recorded the new interest of the women's organization, work with migrants, and the new mission work in Colombia. Amelia Mueller, one of the migrant workers in 1947, wrote in *Missionary News and Notes* of what a migrant camp was like:

A large, attractive house, a well-kept lawn, a large two-car garage, a big chicken house, perhaps a large machine shed or two, and at the edge of the farmyard a tiny one room house of the migrant workers. That, we found, was the typical setup of the farms belonging to the beet growers. . . . Here at least, most of the families had a house to themselves, and most of the growers provided houses that were in good condition. . . . Other workers of which we heard, actually lived in chicken houses. . . . While our primary object in working among the migrants is to bring to them the Gospel of Christ, it is also of tremendous concern to us as Christian workers that conditions be improved for them. [4]

From Colombia, South America, Gerald Stucky wrote,

All of the children that we have thus far are from leper parents and the majority are from Agua de Dios, the leper colony. They are either from evangelical parents or parents who are sympathetic to the evangelical faith. . . . The children range in age from 3 to 21 years. They are poor. Their parents in the colony have an income of about $10 a month, and of that pay us $1.00 a month. We are to receive more children as soon as we have more beds. [5]

The 1950s had the gentle themes of "Pathways to God" and "The Christian Home," and the first optimistic article on missions in Japan.

The 1960s saw the publication of the first official *WMA Manual* and a *Leader's Resource Manual for Young Mission Workers*, but the study lessons faced the harsh confrontations of the world around them: "Race Relations in Reality" and the "Biblical Basis of Non-Resistance."

In the 1970s women were trying to understand the problems and challenges of "Missions at the Crossroads." Another kind of problem and challenge dealt with the role of women in the church. Joyce Shutt wrote in a lesson entitled "Women Toward Freedom and Fulfillment,"

> Women are struggling to discover an identity beyond the role of wife and mother. Many excellent books and articles are devoted to the subject. What emerges from all, whether angry and militant or pensive and objective in tone, is the growing awareness that before anyone, male or female, can be happy and productive, they must first see themselves as a person responsible and self sufficient, contributing to society. The very social and technological institutions which limit women's capacities to become complete persons deny men the same opportunities. [6]

Window to Mission began a series, "A Woman in Mission," which told the story of women in all walks of life in their fulfilling roles. In the 1970s also, when children spent more time in front of a television set than they did at school, Women in Mission printed a bright red brochure which asked, "What is Television Teaching Your Family?"

From the low-caste Indian to the economically abused migrant to the effect of wars and modern technology, the publications of Women in Mission reflected their concerns and interests. The columns in the church papers were their first attempts to publicize their work and their response to missionaries. Originally all their information was given them by the mission board, but soon letters were written to the WMA directly. The vast amount of correspondence entailed to get this information to the local mission societies made it imperative that another way be found to promote their involvement. Two resolutions passed at the 1926 triennial conference launched them into the field of publication. One was the resolution to issue a monthly letter from the Executive Committee to be sent to each local mission group; the other was to establish a Literature Committee in charge of printing pamphlets and brochures which would help to educate their readers and provide another medium of contact with persons in the field.

The monthly letter was christened *Missionary News and Notes* by Susie Schroeder (Mrs. P. R.), who by virtue of her office as secretary of the women's association became its first editor. Susannah Haury continued to call it "the monthly letter," apparently not too satisfied with the name chosen. In the first issue, Susie wrote,

> It is a long recognized fact that we must first know a thing before we will pray for it and when we have begun to pray for it we shall also be willing to sacrifice for it. And that shall be the sole purpose of these "News and Notes," to further missionary interest by imparting information and pleading for the prayers and gifts of our missionary friends. [7]

As with other beginnings, being responsible for this pioneering venture required much creativity and a great deal of time. One of the Schroeder daughters remembers the dining room table was always piled high with papers and letters which the four girls were forbidden to touch. At the beginning, one copy of each issue was mailed to each society with the request that it be read aloud at the meeting so everyone would be informed. The price was five cents per member annually, with a few extra personal subscriptions also available at that price.

For three years the paper was printed in both English and German, with the smaller number of German copies run off on a mimeograph by Susie's husband, the pastor of the Berne church. Rev. Schroeder furnished both stencils and ink, cut the stencils for the paper, worked a half day each month for the issue, and charged the women's association one dollar. Three hundred copies were mailed monthly, each one folded and addressed by hand. During this period *Missionary News and Notes* was partly financed by the sale of metal buttons which were used in making garments for India. The buttons which had been purchased from a firm in Mt. Lake,

Minnesota, were sold at ten cents a dozen for the small size, and fifteen cents a dozen for the large size. In addition to her duties as editor, Susie Schroeder was in charge of button sales.

There was no policy concerning the size of the publication and it varied from issue to issue, as did the grade of paper. Meager references to it in Executive Committee letters seem to indicate that a few copies were always run on good paper to be saved, and the rest didn't matter. The women were amateurs in the publishing business and too caught up in the work and challenge of the present to give much thought to preserving their publications in more artistic shape for the future. With the decision on a standardized six-by-nine-inch size came the further conclusion to do away with the mimeographing, and printed German and English issues appeared monthly. The chairperson of the Literature Committee, F. Luella Krehbiel, suggested that the "Woman's Work" and "Frauenecke" columns be dropped in favor of greater use of their own monthly paper and with less duplication. Arguing that there is great advantage in "ones"[8] (a single publication instead of three), Luella found ready agreement from Hillegonda van der Smissen, German editor, but the Executive Committee was uncertain, and the columns continued "Woman's Work" for three years and "Frauenecke" for six.

The German and English editions appeared separately for seven years until the following announcement in the April 1936 issue stated, "For some time the editor and committee have been considering the advisability of uniting our English and German papers and have concluded to give this change a trial. We have been printing about four times as many English papers as German . . . and the proportion of the English is steadily increasing over the German."[9] An eight-page, bilingual publication was the result. It was not until 1946 that the German was reluctantly dropped because they felt the small number of readers limited to the one language did not justify the additional costs of publishing a

Women's Association publications

dual-language paper.

Helena Siemens of Altona, Manitoba, was appointed to edit a paper called *Unser Missionsblatt* for the benefit of Canadian-German readers. Helena wrote, "The prospects are that our second-generation Mennonites in Canada will not want a paper in the German language. But that is not as important as our religious or spiritual heritage, which we try to save and build up with our papers." [10] *Unser Missionsblatt* was underwritten by the women of the Canadian Conference until the paper suffered financial problems and was discontinued in 1963. After that the column "Frauenseite daheim und draussen" was established in *Der Bote*, and continues.

Missionary News and Notes provided an excellent outlet for missionaries to write very personally about the people with whom they were working and about themselves, knowing that this reading audience was vitally interested in their particular area of work. Societies already well acquainted with their particular missionary families now read first-hand reports from other missionaries whose names and experiences would also become personal, as all were given a turn to tell their stories.

Gerald Stucky wrote, "We are still in language school trying to carry a full schedule although it is difficult to find time enough to study with Judith and Peter to care for at the same time. From our slightly prejudiced viewpoint, we have two unusually good children." [11]

Missionary News and Notes reported in sentence news bits that "Rev. and Mrs. Malcom Wenger and baby Elizabeth had the joy of having Mrs. Wenger's parents for a few weeks' visit during July and August." "Mrs. Thiessen, Mrs. Bauman and Mrs. Unruh went up into the hills with their children to put them into school," and on another such occasion that Christine Marie Duerksen cried when she had to leave for boarding school. [12]

The gentle tribute of a missionary to his wife was published:

The quiet service of a missionary's wife no one appreciates quite as much as her husband. A missionary with a family has responsibilities to his family which he cannot escape. His family is a God-entrusted charge. When his work takes him away from home for weeks at a time, he feels very grateful and happy when his wife largely shoulders the responsibility. I wish herewith to express my indebtedness to Mrs. Unruh for what she does in this respect. Altho she does not go out for village work very much because of home duties, still I feel she does a real service by relieving her husband so that he can give his time to village evangelism. Surely if "they also serve who only stand and wait" then those who serve at home so that others can go out to serve, serve in a very vital sense of the word. While I was out on tour Mrs. Unruh taught Willis Orie and carried him through the first grade so that when we enrolled him at Woodstock School he could go into 1 standard (second grade). It is a relief to me to know my home has not suffered in my absence.

W. F. Unruh [13]

Reliance on prayer and strong belief in its effectiveness were self-evident in the repeated calls for it in their publications through the years. An editorial entitled "Therefore Pray" in the October 1926 issue of *Missionary News and Notes* is typical:

Before all else the world needs men who will pray. "Our way," said a great preacher, "would be to say, 'The harvest truly is plenteous, therefore organize, therefore take a collection, therefore agitate.' Jesus says, 'Therefore pray.'" The missionary society ought to be the great reservoir of the prayer life of the church. [14]

The first "Prayer Cycles" appeared in 1930, and went through several revisions. A similar expanded prayer program with Dorothea Dyck as its editor appeared in 1965; "Prayer Concerns" contained bits of information about missionaries and work of the conference to enable the reader to pray more specifically.

By 1945, at the repeated prodding of WMA secretary Martha Goerz, who was also serving as editor, the Executive Committee was convinced that the editing of the paper had to be given to one individual who would be responsible solely for that work. Joanna Andres (Mrs. H. J.) of Newton was asked to be editor, with Elma Sprunger of Berne, Indiana, responsible for the mailing lists. Joanna promptly redesigned the masthead of the paper and gave it the format it would carry for many years.[15] Her first issue in September 1945 was a tribute to Martha Goerz, her predecessor.

In an effort to increase subscriptions, the Executive Committee passed the following recommendation in 1945: "As a means of securing greater missionary interest we place, next to a consecrated reading of and understanding of the Holy Scriptures, a wider reading of missionary information; and therefore recommend and strongly urge that each mission society subscribe for as many copies of *Missionary News and Notes* as there are families in the church so that every home in the church receives one."[16] Although a few churches subscribed for each family, the total number was disappointingly small.

At intervals through the years, such as in 1947 and 1961, the board of publications suggested that *Missionary News and Notes* merge with *The Mennonite*. Each time the WMA Executive Council weighed the advantages and disadvantages and decided against merger. They were unwilling to give up the close ties with the societies which their paper afforded them, and they felt that no one could provide as much information for their own groups as they could themselves. At one time the executive secretary confided that she felt they (the Board of Publications) "will soon put the skids under our mission paper."[17] Although the organization had been promised space in *The Mennonite* should such consolidation occur, the majority of the women feared they would be absorbed by the larger paper and would lose their identity, and that by such a step they would go backwards.

An observant Canadian reader suggested there was room

for improvement in the appearance of *Missionary News and Notes*. She said it looked just like it did when she was a girl, and she recommended the services of "an art consultant and editorial experts."[18] An unsympathetic secretary told her that would cost money, which they didn't have and couldn't obtain. She wrote, "As we discovered long ago that raising the subscription is not the answer; for an attempt to raise it only 15¢ a year resulted in the prompt drop of 900 subscriptions."[19]

Although the paper was not written for women only, and the information it contained was of worth to any reader, it found little readership outside the women's circles. In an effort to build a larger circulation it was decided to change the style to be more of a family paper and give it a different name. *Missions Today*, printed on fine quality paper and replete with pictures, made its appearance in April 1965. As its predecessor, it provided coverage of missions, both foreign and home, with Anna Sprunger of Berne, Indiana, serving as editor of both papers. She was succeeded by Marie Dyck of Elbing, Kansas, but the results of few added subscribers were again disappointing.

Another crisis occurred when the mission board decided to eliminate the field papers which they had been publishing for each mission area. With this source of information no longer available to the WMA, and with the mission board planning to publish its own composite paper, there was little choice but to discontinue *Missions Today*. With the printing of its last issue in September 1973, *Missions Today* and its forerunner, *Missionary News and Notes*, represented forty-seven years of intense mission promotion by the organization. When *Window to Mission* would make its appearance a year and a half later, it would have a different focus.

How can one set a value on the information learned in the women's publications? Those first short editions, read to the whole group, contained enough inspiration to move the women into actively and enthusiastically supporting mission work. What they learned did not stay in their small groups only; it was shared with the entire congregation in mission programs and in family circles. Teaching of children in Sunday schools and youth groups, a traditional role for women, meant that children of many families heard countless stories of people living and working overseas. The teacher had access to a ready source of material from which to draw, and many can remember the stories that sparked a Sunday school class.

One Kansas society learned about the first native worker in Champa, India, named Joseph Banwar, and they helped support him. As his three children grew, the society provided funds for their education. When the daughter became a doctor, "all mission friends rejoiced," and the society sent her a wristwatch as a graduation present.[20] The personal element was priceless. Continually strengthened by sharing information and goods, the mission society members knew they were agents of the church's outreach.

The Literature Committee

The venture for the women's organization of publishing its own literature began in one of the local groups, the Women's Missionary Society of First Mennonite Church of Bluffton, Ohio. Convinced that having stories available in pamphlet form was a good way of promoting interest, this small group, on behalf of the Middle District, published three brochures: "The Conversion of Garib" by Martha Burkhalter (two for five cents); "What God Hath Wrought" by Rev. and Mrs. E. B. Steiner; and one by E. G. Kaufman entitled "The Present Situation in China" (four cents). Finding the publication business geared more to a larger sponsor than one small society, they offered the continuation of such work to the General Conference Women's Association.

At the triennial session in Berne in 1926 the women officially agreed to enter literature production and appointed their first committee, three of whom had experience in Bluffton: Sara Schultz (Mrs. J. S.) who would serve eighteen years; Dora Quiring (Mrs. J.); and, as chairperson, Minerva Musselman (Mrs. S. M.). The major thrust of the committee then became the publishing of pamphlets and study guides to supplement *Missionary News and Notes* and to provide program and lesson materials for the individual societies. At the end of their first triennial period of existence they reported that of twelve thousand leaflets printed during that period, over ten thousand had reached the homes of people. Of the twelve thousand printed the following year, only about one hundred were still available. That 1930/31 publishing included four thousand Prayer Cycles, three thousand copies of "He Was, He Is, He Will Be" by P. A. Penner, four thousand junior leaflets, and one thousand leaflets describing the Basna Boarding School. Since none were sent out except by request, the record was excellent.

When S. T. Moyer wrote *With Christ on the Edge of the Jungle*, the Literature Committee provided a study guide by Dorothy A. Krehbiel to accompany the book. Their visual aids in the early years included maps of India and China. The maps were available in large and small sizes, with many juniors using the smaller sizes. Study programs accompanied the maps.

Members of the Literature Committee mailed out all materials from their homes. There was no central office distribution until 1947. Each member was also responsible to take materials for sale to district conferences. Sometimes they sold out, and at other times they were to echo the sentiments of the executive secretary who complained, "They don't want literature. They want returned missionaries to give them entertaining travelogues."[21] At one conference a committee member experimented with free literature, but she provided a jar for contributions to the literature fund. At the end of the day her happy conclusion was that many more people had taken leaflets than would have bought them, and she was only one dollar short of meeting the cost.[22]

The Literature Committee was fortified by the opinion of

P. A. Penner who wrote that he just wished the folks at home would keep seven dollars out of every ten dollars that is given for missions, and use it for missionary literature. [23]

Brief missionary biographies appeared in *Missionary News and Notes* in 1940, and in 1947 the committee decided to publish biographies in loose-leaf form of all the missionaries, country by country. They began with enthusiasm, producing attractive and descriptive life histories, but they found great frustration in the slow cooperation from the missionaries themselves who were supposed to supply the necessary information. They also found it difficult to keep up with the changing staffs in each area, so when the Foreign Mission Board offered to continue the program, they gladly turned over all their available materials.

To make study fun and challenging, the Literature Committee proposed unique methods—a missionary achievement test, mission quizzes at conference meetings, a local historian to keep each group up to date, snappy book resumés, a missionary parade, and a booklet of missionary games. They provided *A Guide Book and Catalogue for Missionary Societies* which had a complete listing of books available for the asking for serious study.

In some areas there was a growing recognition that many of the women in church were better informed than the men concerning missions. From Central District comes the story of a man who was asked what his church contributed to foreign missions. "I don't know," he replied. "I forgot to ask my wife." [24]

In the 1970s one missionary said her favorite itineration was to the mission societies. "At least they know who you are," she commented. [25]

The Literature Committee not only promoted Mennonite materials but also made good use—too much, some said—of other Protestant publications dealing with the area of missions in general. They also promoted plays and devotions which were published by other women's organizations, and a kind of friendship grew which would later result in the promotion of inter-Mennonite and interdenominational endeavors.

Although the committee tried to make use of familiar writers, the results were not always what they should have been. Eleanor Camp, office secretary, wrote to a member of the Literature Committee encouraging her to visit home-mission areas and write about them. "The missionaries cannot be depended on to write. They have too much to do, and they are too close to things so that they lose their perspective, and worse still their sense of wonder. When they write, they preach at the reader instead of giving us pictures of a people as alive as we are to the possibilities of life on its upper levels, and as keenly aware of its frustrations when not properly motivated. We get better sermons at home." [26]

In an attempt to have circles responsible for building their local church libraries, the Literature Committee encouraged the establishment of Memorial Library books in memory of deceased members. The committee offered to provide gummed labels to be put in these books at three cents apiece and they compiled a list of 100 good books for those who wanted help in the selection of worthwhile mission materials. The society at Drake, Saskatchewan, was the first to establish such a library. A number of other groups responded, and there were undoubtedly more who carried out the idea without writing for the helps.

A loan library provided another helpful means of getting good books into the local churches. The WMA bought about 150 recommended books which could be borrowed for three weeks at ten cents a book. When a full-time executive secretary was employed, all these aforementioned materials were available from the central office, and some of the load was lifted from the shoulders of the Literature Committee.

Almost from the beginning, study guides were provided annually to help local groups with different areas of learning. At the start they were heavily foreign-mission oriented, but as time went along they began to touch personal growth and Christian development as well. In 1951 a free copy of the year's guide was given to each society as an experiment in making the literature more available and useful and to acquaint them with the work of the Literature Committee. That practice continued with additional copies available at a small fee, until with the appearance of *Window to Mission* the "Resource for Adult Study" became a regular feature in that publication.

Stella Kreider (Mrs. A. E.), a member of the Literature Committee and an ardent promoter of inter-Mennonite cooperation, endorsed the suggestion of friends in 1945 that perhaps the time had come for a women's inter-Mennonite paper "to help unite us in thought." One suggestion for a name might be "The Mennonite Woman." She wrote:

It need not carry missionary news, since other church publications are doing that for us. It might carry a page for young mothers relating to child health and care; a section for the hospital nurse; news and comments of interest primarily to women; a section on the kitchen, household hints, sectional recipes, balanced meals; a needlework page which specialized in arts and crafts such as quilting, rug making and knitting of lace; peculiar folklore and stories sought out by the English department in our colleges; a poetry page; some good editorials especially appealing to Mennonite women; a page of devotional Bible study for spiritual growth . . . an exchange column where a Mennonite woman or girl in one part of the country might find a job in some other locality if she so chooses. [27]

No action followed her suggestion. When in 1976/77 the recommendation was again made that a Meetinghouse edition of *Voice*, the publication of the Missionary and Service Commission of The Mennonite Church, and *Window to Mission* be tried, it again came to nought.

On behalf of the Board of Publications in 1949, B. Bargen recommended that the WMA do all its printing and marketing through the publications board, rather than through independent agencies as they had been doing. He added, "(They, WMA) operate their work on such a small margin as to be a very small profit and a very large headache."[28] He was unquestionably right about the small profit. Because of their penny-pinching, women's organizations were a source of irritation to the business world, not only in Mennonite circles, but in other Protestant organizations as well. The claim was repeatedly made, and with good justification, that they underpaid their workers to such an extent that all normal wage schedules suffered by comparison. Women's societies had shoestring budgets and much of their work was volunteer. It was not until the 1970s that the WMA, under the prompting of the Division of Administration, brought the salaries of their employees into line with General Conference policy. Even then there was much continued volunteer labor and personal payment of expenses. Certainly the Literature Committee never functioned with the idea of making a profit, and meeting expenses was the highest hope of their publishing enterprises. By 1953 they discontinued their own printing and publishing, as Bargen suggested.

When *Window to Mission* came into being, the decision was made to put their publications under one cover, the "ones" F. Luella Krehbiel had talked about many years before. As a result, the study guides were incorporated with the periodical. Because *Window to Mission* came as a quarterly insert in *The Mennonite* it was sent to 16,000 subscribers, most of whom did not belong to mission circles; thus the Literature Committee needed to focus lessons with that in mind, a process actually begun earlier. A broader reading public widened the field of interest, so combined with lessons which still featured overseas and home missions were lessons dealing with learning and interpersonal relationships. Some of the lessons were issues studied in conjunction with the work of the Commission on Education, and some were a reflection of life at hand.

"Welcome to *Window to Mission*! May it be a place where we learn and share and mature in following our risen Lord!"[29] These opening words of the editorial in the first issue were indicative of the direction the new publication would take under the editorship of Muriel Stackley and her successor, Jeannie Zehr. Two of the pages of each issue still provided the contact between women's groups of the General Conference, but a larger portion of the paper directed itself to all within the church.

4 the fund raisers

"There have been three potent forces in the women's campaign for missions: self-sacrifice; organization; accumulation - by littles." [1]

This description by a Presbyterian woman of the organizations with which she was familiar is accurate of Mennonite women as well. What held the mission societies together in the early years? Certainly it was not their wealth. As women met in homes through most of those years, they felt the overwhelming call to share what they had with those who had greater needs. They considered the missionaries, for whom they had the greatest respect, to be their representatives in parts of the world they never expected to see; and they automatically assumed that they had an obligation to support these representatives with money and goods. The Mennonite church had become part of the great Protestant missionary movement in the nineteenth century, and the women, deliberately or unconsciously, joined the ranks of women's circles.

Like their Protestant counterparts in eastern United States who formed Female Societies which asked for a cent a week for missions from their members, Mennonite women began with humble financial goals. They had little money to call their own. There were few wage earners among them in the early years. Only the Eastern District talked about numbers of employed women. For the most part married women were not handlers of the family funds; that was for the men to do. Consequently they began thinking in the "littles," the extras they might call their own.

Sunday egg money was one such source. Some farm woman who depended on income from eggs for cash probably suggested the idea. The Executive Committee promoted the idea in the pages of *Missionary News and Notes*. "We would recommend that as many as can, use their Sunday egg money for the Lord's cause," read an appeal in the December 1926 issue.

From Eastern District comes the story of two women who picked and cleaned dandelion greens to serve with bacon dressing at a dinner for a quarterly conference of pastors which met at their church. The women had little money with which to work and the pastors could ill afford a fair donation for the cost of the meal. The women were pleased if the donation covered the cost of the meal, and were really delighted if they made a dollar or two profit. [2]

Mission sales which combined the homemaker's skills of sewing and baking were the chief source of money-making for many groups, particularly in Canada. From British Columbia comes this incident of stretching pennies into dollars with similar accounts, also true of other early Canadian societies:

Every beginning is hard, and so it was also when poor Mennonite settlers came to Coghlan, B.C. in 1934. Wherever Mennonites settle, there soon grows the desire for Christian fellowship. However, there was no money. The women were called upon to raise money by sewing articles and selling them, thus establishing a church construction fund with the proceeds. Six ladies began the work. Each one donated 25 cents. For this amount material was ordered from Eaton's. Eaton's also sent along several remnants. Each woman donated one flour sack and the ladies' aid from Yarrow, B.C. favoured us with two dollars and one pair of pillowcases. When the English neighbors heard about our work, they too made a donation. A beginning had been made and God granted growth and prosperity. Our first auction, 1936, brought 83 dollars. [3]

When the first provincial meeting was held in Yarrow five years later, the offering amounted to $6.20. Of this amount they gave $3.00 to the Red Cross, $3.00 to the needy, and twenty cents for the necessary paper expenses. In contrast, the provincial annual meeting offering in 1978 was $2,208.26, and their yearly contributions were $23,192.79. [4]

In Kansas, the women of the Hoffnungsau church were assigned to sew eighty garments for the boys at Mahaudi school in India, and they had barely enough money to buy material for their project. Their president said that "with a heavy heart" they discussed ways and means of financing their projects and came up with the decision to try a mission sale. "The next time the ministers and deacons of the congregation met we took our problems and propositions to them asking for their permission in this venture. After thorough consideration they gave us permission to go ahead with the project, with the proviso that it was to be conducted on the outside of the church building." [5] Undaunted by the half-hearted endorsement, the ladies strung lines from one big shade tree to another and hung up the items they had made for sale. "The ministers helped us as best they could," was the polite comment of the president. A large crowd came and the sale was such a success that it became an annual event for years.

Raffles were held by many Canadian societies, and that met with some disapproval from the WMA executives. After a visit to Canada, Marie Lohrentz, WMA president, said she did hope they would find some other way to raise money, although she held a high opinion of the people she met. "I never met women who were so willing, so eager, so genuinely interested as these. I am enjoying the contacts thoroughly."[6] In spite of executive disapproval, the number of mission sales and raffles grew and continued for many years, and provided the chief source of income for women's groups. These mission sales were the forerunners of the MCC relief auctions which would later replace many of them.

Closely allied with sewed items was the preparation of food in one form or another for fund raising. Most societies could point to food served at dinners, fowl suppers, borscht suppers, or bake sales. Booths at community sales, country fairs, celebrations, and even a wolf hunt provided a service and added income for local mission groups. Some of the methods of raising money seem only to have been means of making fund giving enjoyable, not more profitable, and they were viewed with displeasure by others. "We had a silent bake sale," wrote one woman. "One would bake something and give it to the next name on the list, then she would put in the jar what she thought it was worth and make something and give it to the next name. It was a lot of fun."[7] Critics pointed out that anyone could make money by donating the items and then buying them back, but they discounted the pleasure such exchanges frequently provided.

Sometimes a group became known for one speciality, such as making noodles. One group for years made hundreds of pounds of peppernuts which they sold during the holiday season, while another group sold dressed ducks at Thanksgiving time. Others made zwieback, New Year's cookies, and fancy breads. Poppy seed rolls and rollkuchen were eagerly awaited by the communities which looked forward to annual bake sales. One group made Easter egg candy in all flavors—nut, vanilla, coconut, peanut butter, and cherry—which they sold to nearby factories.

When quilting skills began to disappear, many groups added commercial quilting to their ways of raising money, although both knotting comforters and quilting for relief continued. It should be pointed out that virtually every money-making project was done countless times "for free" to

Local group at work

the local congregations, who casually accepted it as their due.

Less enjoyable were the sales of vanilla or wall cleaners and assorted products. Different names were assigned to projects, such as birthday money, sacrifice money, dime projects, sunshine funds, basket funds, black purse offerings, and many more. Mite boxes, a method copied from other denominations, were used by many groups; usually designated in advance for some particular project, these frequently brought sizeable thank offerings. Some of the methods of fund raising were obviously designed just to be creative approaches to giving. Women knew from the beginning that they would be making a donation, but they wanted some social enjoyment while they did so.

An incident which calls to mind the biblical account of the widow's mite deals with one group of older ladies, most of whom were on social security. They were having a difficult time meeting the WMA assignments but were determined to do so. The husband of one offered to give them the required funds, but they refused. They wanted to do it all by themselves, and by careful saving they did. The same sort of independent pride characterized other groups in other years when it was only determination and commitment which made giving possible.

"Dear Mr. ____," began a letter received by the WMA in February 1928.

> Since a number of sisters in our congregation have decided to do something for Missions but we have nothing to start with, we are asking whether you would please loan us $10.00 for this purpose. We promise to return the money from the proceeds of our first sale.
>
> With kind greetings,
Sincerely,

_____"[8]

The WMA loaned them the funds. It is interesting to speculate why they didn't feel free to ask the brethren in their own congregation for a loan.

Programs to which the congregation and community were invited provided not only sizable offerings for missions but teaching about the mission program. Frequently guest speakers and films provided the input, with missionaries on furlough being the favorites. Another favorite on this order was the meal prepared with the help of the missionary as typical of the country in which she had worked.

One successful venture for many was in the printing of local cookbooks. Such a project was a natural for good Mennonite cooks who were always looking for one more interesting recipe.

The most common and probably most consistent giving came from free-will offerings and pledges through the years. The "littles" sometimes meant $1.27 a month and a yearly total of $15.50, carefully divided and contributed according to their plan, as reported by a group in Oregon. [9] This method of voluntary contribution was encouraged and promoted by WMA executives consistently through the years, but their influence seems to have been minor. Using one's hands seemed to have provided more reward than just handling money.

For the first thirty-one years of its existence, the women's organization had no budget. Money was allotted as it was donated, but there was no overall plan for giving. The workload of the organization had become so heavy that it could no longer be handled in the homes of the committee members, so in 1947 the WMA acquired an office and its first employee, Eleanor Camp. She was designated as their treasurer, but for all practical purposes she provided the functions of an executive secretary. This new arrangement indicated an annual budget. The treasurer carefully account- ed for all funds donated and published them regularly in *Missionary News and Notes*. It is not clear whether in the beginning the women's organization asked for specific projects from the mission board, or whether the board merely assigned a portion as a basis for a project. In either event, the idea of projects early became deeply ingrained. This proved to be a mixed blessing as local groups insisted they wanted to contribute to projects, not budget. Treasurer Frieda Regier said, "We soon will have nothing but 'specials' and 'extras' if this keeps on. . . . Seems to me if all would give to the Gen'l Fund all the 'specials' wouldn't be necessary." [10] She worried because they were always in the red in their expense account. The mission board had offered to pay their expenses, should they need help, and although they resisted originally, there were times when they had to bend their pride to ask for help. Funds for maintenance lacked the charm of special projects, a fact of life even the mission board had to live with, but a later executive secretary of the WMA pointed out, "Unspec- tacular budget items can be the Lord's work." [11]

In the early years of the conference organization, the Canadian missionary societies were not given assignments because "they more than had their hands full, as they did so much for our immigrant brothers and sisters." [12] Even as late as 1946 the president of the WMA who had visited in Canada wrote, "Some of our Canadian societies do mostly relief now, for it is *so* close to them, for they only came over between 1920-30." [13] The needs at their front door were of first importance, and since many of the helpers were not wealthy there was little left after caring for their neighbors.

As finances and conditions improved, Canadians were given assignments also. In 1930 Sophia Krehbiel (Mrs. G. A.) became their first WMA sewing supervisor. In *The History of Canadian Women in Mission*, Mrs. Krehbiel describes her introduction to the work: "The WMA consulted Benj. Ewert to recommend someone, so that is how I got in. My first duty was to get a list of all the Canadian societies. Rev. B. Ewert and Rev. J. J. Thiessen were a big help in this. Rev. Thiessen also helped to make out the questionnaire. From these (questionnaires) I gave reports at the Canadian annual conference, also at the triennial of the General Conference." [14] Ewert was the "reise prediger" ("traveling minister") and he proved a real friend, as the WMA called on him repeatedly for help.

After her visitation in Ontario in 1946, Aganetha Fast told the WMA executives, "In all places they had women getting together, but none were really organized. They had a Vorsteherin, and a Schreiberin, but the money they collected or in some way gathered, all was given to the treasurer of the Church. It seemed to me, that here was where the crux of the situation lay. The Brethren did not quite appreciate in a few churches that the women would disperse their funds." [15]

Mrs. Krehbiel was named as assistant treasurer in Canada two years after appointment as adviser, and societies were advised to send their contributions through her. She found many of the groups less than cooperative, probably through no fault of their own, as their funds had to be given through their church treasurer who forwarded them to the provincial and General Conferences. She wrote to the Executive Committee, "Some of the women probably would become independent if they were given a chance by the men." [16] Others told her they didn't want to bother handling money or making reports because "Wir sind noch sehr alt modisch." [17] ("We are still very old fashioned.")

In 1954 the WMA treasurer told the committee,

> Up to the present time we have never been able to take any credit toward our WMA budget from the gifts of the Canadian Women's societies, except for the few gifts that were sent direct to us. This is because Rev. J. J. Thiessen held a pretty tight rein on all these contributions and counted them as part of the money flowing direct to the Foreign Mission Board. . . . Miss Edna Ruth Mueller, the assistant conference treasurer now assures me that we can apply the women's contributions from Canada on our own WMA budget. . . . I am very happy about this arrangement and hope we can find acceptance for it among members of the board. [18]

An item in their 1957 minutes read, "It was decided that the new Canadian Central treasurer be asked if he could separate the Women's treasury reports from the total." [19] In spite of optimism, funds from Canada continued to come in often without designation that they were contributed by women, and in 1958 the WMA president was still hoping that all women's funds would be given to them.

When funds from Canada finally did come in regularly, contributions from Canadian women, once carefully shielded because of their financial status, soon surpassed their United States sisters in per capita giving. Their strongest area of support, like that of the women's organization in the beginning, was in the field of overseas mission. Mrs. Krehbiel continued as the chief Canadian representative to the General Conference in one capacity or another for twenty-eight years.

One of the most systematic forms of giving to the WMA was designed by the Central District. Vinora Salzman, one of the planners, gives this account:

> They (Central District) appointed a committee to arrange some way in which our giving could be more systematic. Naomi Vercler and I met again and again - I recall one night we spent the greater part of the night struggling with this problem - we met in Fort Wayne one whole day and finally came forth with a plan: We took the budget of the General Conference for the year, took our percentage for

our district - divided this into 3 sections & then divided the places for giving into 4 quarters. It was difficult at first but we feel has been quite successful. [20]

Central District continues to lead in balanced giving today by following this plan.

With increased giving and more organization came the demand for making of records and reports, not a favorite activity with many. Although told by the Executive Committee that the information contained in the reports helped them plan more efficiently and with a greater degree of accuracy than without that vital information, women complained and many refused to cooperate. Greatest resistance seems to have come from the Northern District and the Canadian Conference. By 1935 the WMA decided there was not too much point in sending questionnaires to Canada because so few were returned, so they asked Mrs. Krehbiel and Rev. Ewert to make evaluations. Years later when there was greater interest in conference activity, Mrs. Krehbiel commented, "I find at our Conf. that the ones returning their paper are the ones that attend with delegates." [21]

One group informed the Northern District adviser that the Bible said the left hand wasn't supposed to know what the right hand was doing, so obviously there was no need of record keeping.

From the Pacific District a protester wrote, "It is easier for me to pack and give it to the Salvation Army, where they say 'Thank you,' and I say 'you're welcome,' no reports, no weighing, no price." [22] With characteristic tact, Executive Secretary Dorothea Dyck wrote, "It is a matter of not bragging on ourselves but of accurate reporting. . . . I wish that there were ways of evaluating other things. For example the Christian witness of the individual members of a society. The elderly people encouraged, the prayer support and the mission study, the burdens lifted from those who are over burdened, the books read which have enriched our lives, etc. Some of these things just can't be measured and so the nearest we can come to it is pounds of MCC relief." [23]

The financial status of women today contrasts sharply with the pioneer days of the organization. During the last two decades when women began to move into the field of employment in larger numbers, local groups were finding fewer women available to do the work of fund raising by providing the expected services. Some employed women gave money instead of labor, some dropped out completely, and others continued as active members.

At the same time, the "littles" of yesterday yielded to impressive contributions with over a half-million dollars given by local groups in 1979. The total does not include the value of large donations in material aid as well. Approximately two-fifths of the total went directly to district, provincial, and General Conference organizations. Local churches and communities and Mennonite Central Committee received sizable contributions also.

Today the women's organization finds itself divided on the issue of money. Voices are calling for an end to being fund raisers and suggesting that the time has come for women to concentrate on the personal healing needed by many and to which women have great gifts to offer, the problems of broken homes, divorce, loneliness, and the issues involving employed women and the church. One woman writes,

> I think the women's groups should take the women's revolution seriously—men's clubs and women's groups have a place, but only for limited activities, and it would need a specific purpose. Right now the new generation of married women need help at working at the real problems—how to combine careers and homemaking, how to organize a household so father can be in charge of children and household duties. We are fighting a whole society structure and we need the best brains and ideas to work out solutions. . . . Our whole organization would take on a different purpose if we tried to fit into the church pattern—give the money-raising and treasury bit back to the church altogether—we don't *need* that to feel important anymore, nor do we need that power! [24]

On another note a former WMA president wrote, "Women have a lot of energy and many feel rewarded when they see their money doing something special. As of now it seems that too many still need this outlet, however, I believe this will eventually need to be changed."[25]

From another former president comes a strong avowal that money has its place.

Growing up in a church with a large and active women's missionary society, I early learned that the monthly offering was an important part of their program. Deep interest in the cause of missions prompted a voluntary support of the work. This must still hold true for Women in Mission of 1980. In early years the famed 'Sunday egg money' was given for missions, but today women, especially wage-earners, are able to give much more generously. Needs today are broader and involvement takes many different forms, but the principle is the same: Where there is interest and concern, financial support is the natural result. Women in Mission would lose much of its impact if it should decide to *study* Overseas Missions and Home Ministries, Education and Publication, and other projects, but *fall short of giving them financial support*."[26]

Missionary Pension Fund

Through the years there were many special funds, three of which are of unique interest: Missionary Pension Fund, Memorial Loan Fund, and the Taiwan Choir - World Conference Fund. The earliest was the pension fund.

The mission board, in 1926, passed a resolution to accept a plan entitled "Missionaries' Pensions." The trustees referred to it more commonly as "Incapacitated Missionaries' Fund" or "Incapacitated Missionary Fund."[27]

The fund grew slowly, and that it grew at all must be attributed, in large part, to the Women's Missionary Association which adopted it as a part of its projects in 1935. All members were asked to contribute "2 cents a week and a prayer" for missionary pensions. By 1945 over two-thirds of the receipts for the conference pension fund came from the WMA. This did not include contributions from Canadian women, since at this time their gifts were still not credited to the WMA. The organization picked up the project with the intent of making it an endowment fund, with the board of trustees investing the funds at the then current rate of 2 to 4 percent interest annually. By 1945 the fund stood at $22,600.61.

An exchange of letters in their Executive Committee round robin in 1952 reveals that the trustees were becoming increasingly impatient with handling the fund separately, and suggested that the WMA give them complete control. WMA President Lohrentz wrote, "As far as Mr. D_____'s letter takes it they are ready to start 'giving away' the Pension Fund right now. . . . Mr. E_____ has asked quite pointedly several times to turn the whole fund over to his committee."[28] The WMA secretary, torn with indecision, responded, "I don't know whether it is wise to put up a protest of this nature, or whether to meekly leave it up to them, trusting in the Lord's leading."[29] Lohrentz wasn't about to give up without a fight, as she answered, "This thing of a policy for Pension Fund is getting nowhere fast, for they do not seem to understand just what we want and simply treat it as a matter over which they have the say-so. It seems to me that it would be best to get a *com. of women* to formulate a policy and then if we want to bring that before the conf. (1953) it could be included in the agenda there."[30]

Before the 1953 conference, the WMA had recommended to the mission board that the interest be made available for use. However, the amount was not large enough to pay all pensions, so the mission board made the following motion which was presented to the WMA executives:

Moved that the annual receipts of two cents per person per week be added to the interest from accumulated pension fund, to make possible more adequate pension payment to such retired missionaries as are not under the Presbyterian Ministers' plan. And that with the approval of the Executive Committee of the Women's Missionary Association, the Board of Missions be privileged to draw upon the principle in case of special need for retired missionaries not under the Presbyterian Ministers' plan. [31]

The Executive Committee agreed to the motion, but when it was read at the WMA triennial session in Oregon, the women refused to go along. In a rare display of independence, and rejection of the Board of Mission's and their own Executive Committee's leading, they argued that this was not the purpose for which they had been collecting the funds, and that they ought to do more thinking before they accepted it. A motion to restudy the recommendation and delay voting failed, but an amendment that the fund be built to $80,000, as permanent endowment, carried. ($65,000 was available at the time of the motion.)

In 1976 the Commission on Overseas Mission and the Commission on Home Ministries added sizable amounts to the retirement program, which today is called "Missionary Supplementary Retirement Fund." Interest from the Women in Mission endowment is also used annually to supplement retirement income, and many local mission societies continue to contribute to it.

Memorial Loan Fund

Women of Canada were meeting together at the Canadian Conference in a loose organization for several years before they officially became WMA Canadian Conference. In the 1943 meetings at Langham, Saskatchewan, Rev. J. J. Thiessen recommended to them that they establish a "Margaret Toews Scholarship" at the German-English academy, to honor the memory of the late Mrs. David Toews and to assist a girl in attending school there. The stipend would be $100 annually for a three-year period and it was set up as a revolving fund. If, however, the girl decided to go into full-time mission work, the debt would be canceled automatically. The project was picked up by the Saskatchewan and

Manitoba WMAs and continued as provincial projects, with Esther Patkau and Helen Kornelson as its first two recipients.

When Martha Goerz died, the WMA received the following suggestion: "This matter might surprise you, but while reading the Canadian leaflet and the report on that "Stipendium" for Mrs. David Toews a thought came to me. With Mrs. Goerz' recent passing and remembering her tireless labors and also Mrs. S. S. Haury's, how could we keep their memories alive among our societies when those of us who are active now will have retired, and this project of the Canadian ladies stood out to me as a challenge."[32] Her challenge took concrete form, and a fund first call the *Haury-Goerz Scholarship Fund* and later known as *Memorial Loan Fund* was set up. Its stated purpose was to aid young women preparing for full-time Christian service. Since the Canadian fund applied to Canadian girls only, this one would be for United States girls. The applicant was to have at least one year of college or its equivalent, a recommendation from the school she had attended, as well as a recommendation from her General Conference home church. The tuition would apply only to a recognized Mennonite school and was available for three years, and she was to serve subsequently in conference mission or church work. The money was to be paid back within five years of entrance into her area of work.

The fund grew, but not one person applied for a loan. Eight years after the suggestion for a loan fund was made, the entire amount of money was turned over to the mission board.

World Conference - Taiwan Choir Fund

Mennonite World Conference (MWC) met in Wichita, Kansas, in 1978. For the first time in its history, the conference had a travel fund for overseas people who were financially unable to come without such assistance. All the travel scholarships were given to men who had been selected by their own church bodies. Because none of the money was allotted to women, the MCC Task Force on Women began to raise funds to bring overseas women. The conference presidium agreed to match funds if $10,000 were raised by the Task Force. General Conference Women in Mission contributed $2,000 of that sum.

Another involvement in MWC came when Martha Vandenberg, missionary in Taiwan, wrote asking Women in Mission if it would be willing to sponsor a tour of a Taiwan women's choir through Mennonite communities in the United States and Canada in conjunction with an appearance at the world conference. Choir members would pay their travel to and from Taiwan.

Women in Mission (WM) enthusiastically embarked on the proposed project. The organization made plans for the choir's travel by bus in the two countries, with most of the lodging during the month's tour to be provided by Mennonite families.

A world conference fund was included in the budget for two years. Offerings to be taken at the concerts would supplement the budget receipts. Expenses for the month's travel were correctly estimated by Women in Mission, but they underestimated the generous offerings where programs were given. WM gave all the proceeds above expenses to projects in Taiwan, including:

Retreat expenses for pastors' wives and missionary women

Youth retreat

Seminary expenses for women students in Taiwan

Church loans for Taiwan

Expenses for a Taiwanese student at Goshen College

Money to be used by a Taiwanese woman delegate to attend the 1980 Asia Conference

COM overseas wives' travel fund[33]

The experience in transcontinental fellowship could be judged a success on all counts.

5 auxiliary

aux•il′ia•ry: conferring help or aid; assistant; supporting; subsidiary; also, additional

Webster's New Collegiate Dictionary

Before the constitution of the General Conference was revised in 1950, there was no mention of the women's organization being in any way a part of the conference. The conference Coordinating Committee consulted the executive officers of the WMA as to how they wished to be identified. The following recommendation was made by the women:

Resolved that the Women's Missionary Association be considered an auxiliary to the General Conference. [1]

Nine years later there was an attempt to incorporate existing auxiliaries into one of the conference boards. This was at a time when the missionary association was working on a revision of its constitution. A letter from the mission board recommended that the WMA include in the constitution a closer working relationship with the mission board. Executive Committee members were asked to attend a joint meeting in Chicago to discuss details with the board which had proposed several points for discussion: (1) Total autonomy for WMA was assured. (2) A new relationship should make possible closer participation by WMA with Board of Missions. (3) Provision could be made for joint meetings at the Council of Boards meetings. (4) Cooperate specifically in special areas in which both were already involved, as in the production of literature. (5) *Missionary News and Notes* would continue. (6) WMA might give leadership in project development. (7) Board of Missions could use the contacts WMA had with districts and local groups. (8) Development of work with children. (9) Special combined service projects. [2]

The joint meeting was held in Chicago on March 14-15, 1960, and at that meeting the women expressed a fear of being "swallowed up" [3] if their auxiliary status was removed. The board assured them that would not happen; they could retain their independence and still relate to the Boards of Education and Christian Service as they now did. In July the women's association issued a preliminary statement of reorganization in which they said, "Complying with the wish of the Executive Committee of the Conference to have all auxiliary organizations affiliated with some Conference board, our Women's Missionary Association, in executive session on July 13, 1960, agreed to accept the invitation of the Board of Missions to cooperate more closely with them in their work, and to share in their overall planning as opportunity offers." [4]

If there was a shift in strategy or program after that point, it is difficult to detect. Members of the conference office staffs worked together on projects, but they had done that before the reorganization as well. The biggest percentage of budget was allotted to the mission board, but that was nothing new. The women recognized that being an official part of the board meant they would have to contribute to the expenses of the General Conference, as did the board. They were unwilling to do that, guarding jealously every dollar given them by the societies. It was unquestionably one of the factors in their clinging to the auxiliary position. History gave them no assurances that once they gave up control of their funds they would be accepted as equal. The new reorganization proposal appears to have been largely an agreement on paper. One wonders how different the history of women's work in the churches and conference might have been had either the WMA or the mission board pursued seriously a program of closer affiliation.

The auxiliary status was subject to debate for many years. In order to have any position with the conference at all, the women felt it necessary to declare themselves an auxiliary, and there is no reason to think it was an unwelcome status. In one early minor disagreement with the board, the women's Executive Committee found real pleasure in the independence being an auxiliary accorded them; they were free to give money to projects the board suggested, or withhold it, and it obviously felt good to decide for themselves. They had felt the urgency of having the Foreign Mission Board officially recognize their existence as they were actively promoting the mission program, but in an early reference to their lack of being recognized by the General Conference proper, Susannah Haury suggested that wasn't all bad because they could be "more unhindered in our movements."[5]

Much depended on the various mission boards. Sometimes the women were welcomed at meetings and their opinions solicited, and at other times the board hardly tolerated their presence. On one occasion the WMA treasurer Frieda Regier Entz expressed uneasiness about the board's actions, "especially after the way they have been acting here of late, having a number of 'closed sessions' as tho they don't want us in on all of it, as tho they do not quite trust us."[6] Her letter implies only the women were excluded, but that is open to question.

Officers of the WMA were usually permitted to listen to the board meetings, but when they first wrote asking whether the chairperson of their Literature Committee could be allowed to attend in order to gain first-hand information, that caused quite a stir. The board did agree to her attending, but added, "I believe it would be well to discuss this at our meeting, so we have a clear understanding about this in the future." [7] The WMA president told her committee, "I am glad we sent the letter and have clarity on it without getting some of the rest of us disqualified—however that may happen at the meeting when it is discussed." [8] Although they were presumably not disqualified, she was to report again four years later that she had "heard rumblings that we are doing too much of it." [9] (That is, attending board meetings.)

When Eleanor Camp became the first employee of the WMA in 1947 she was not an official member of their Executive Committee. After the annual Council of Boards meetings she commented, "I can recall the time at the Bloomington sessions, when I, who did not belong to anything officially, was left dangling out in the lobby during Board sessions, except when the Committee members wanted some typing done. I resolved then that that was it so far as I was concerned; I could spend my time more profitably at the office." [10]

By the late 1960s and 1970s there was increasing question about where the organization stood within the General Conference, and growing dissatisfaction with being by-passed when they wanted to be more actively involved. WMA President Naomi Lehman expressed the deep feelings of the council when she reported, "We want to feel we 'belong,' that we are a functional part of the General Conference, not merely an appendage." [11] During her term of office, new understanding of the meaning of *auxiliary* would evolve.

Africa Inter-Mennonite Mission Auxiliary

Mission interest became evident in the Central Conference of Mennonites and among the congregations of the Defense-less Mennonite Conference (now Evangelical Mennonite Conference) in the period beginning about 1890. In 1905 the Central Conference appointed a Foreign Mission Commit-

African mother and child

tee, sending a couple to work in the territory of the African Inland Mission. In 1907 the Defenseless Conference took similar action. Due to disagreement with the African Inland Mission, both discontinued this work in 1910.

After the discontinuance of the work in British East Africa, the two conferences began action to unite their mission activities. The United Mennonite Board of Missions was organized at Meadows, Illinois, in 1911; on January 23, 1912, the name was changed to *Congo Inland Mission*. [12]

It was not until 1943 that the General Conference became an affiliate member of the Congo Inland Mission (CIM), and it was another four years before the women's association joined the CIM Auxiliary. Their official invitation from the president of the auxiliary read: "Moved and passed that the Women's Foreign and Home Missionary Society of the General Conference be invited to appoint an official representative on the Ladies' Auxiliary of the C.I.M." [13] The invitation was accepted and WMA appointed their president,

Marie Lohrentz, as their first delegate.

The Auxiliary Board then consisted of three women, one from each conference. In 1950 the General Conference women asked for one more board member because of their larger number of constituents. Their request was granted. At their meetings, however, there were always more missionaries in attendance than board members, as well as other guests, and their influence was strong. A special effort was made to include pastors' wives in the area in which the board was meeting, which resulted in even larger numbers at board meetings, with everyone free to take part. Eventually a sort of backlash developed which in 1978 led to spirited discussion on whether Auxiliary Board meetings should be closed to all outsiders. In the official minutes of April 24, 1978, they record: "The April meeting will involve primarily the Women's Auxiliary Executive Committee. They will deal with allocations and projections. The October meeting will probably have lots of missionaries present and will be open to observers who want to come."

In their initial membership, WMA's understanding of what membership meant, particularly as it related to financial matters, was inconsistent. The WMA told the auxiliary that they would support financially only those items which were part of what they called the maintenance of the mission, that is, regular budget, and that their contributions would be given through the General Conference Foreign Mission Board to help them meet their large commitment (70-76 percent) for the budget. They would be willing, however, to help with whatever material aid beyond budget was needed. Consequently, the annual reports of the Ladies' Auxiliary showed much larger contributions by the women of the Evangelical Mennonite Church and Evangelical Mennonite Brethren.

Nevertheless, even material aid meant cash for nonbudget items such as sewing materials to be made into garments and supplies, and as early as her first year at auxiliary meeting, the WMA president pledged $500 for the sewing, and an additional $50 to pay shipping costs to Africa. [14] So in actual practice they were contributing both to budget and to extras, but the women of the Evangelical Mennonite Brethren and Evangelical Mennonite Church were accepting responsibility for the bulk of the auxiliary budget. This understandably led to some dissatisfaction. The WMA promoted the various projects of the CIM Auxiliary, toward which individual societies could contribute, in *Missionary News and Notes*, but this had nothing to do with their official obligations. Precisely when they did accept a proportionate share of the auxiliary budget is not clear; evidently it was a gradual turnover. By 1974 the WMA was contributing 60 percent of the auxiliary budget.

All decisions of the Women's Auxiliary (in 1956 the name was changed from Ladies' Auxiliary to Women's Auxiliary) were subject to approval by the Congo Inland Mission Board. The WMA office secretary said, "Policy is never formulated at these meetings; it is simply announced." [15] Dorothea Dyck served one term as president of the auxiliary, the only General Conference woman to serve as executive officer.

One of the most rewarding experiences with the CIM Auxiliary was the sponsorship of a delegation of four women to Congo (Zaire) in 1971. Women of the Evangelical Mennonite Church and the Evangelical Mennonite Brethren appointed one delegate each, and the General Conference appointed two, choosing one married and one single woman. The WMA president informed the conference,

> The Congo Inland Mission came into being in 1911, and our General Conference began a program of cooperation with CIM in finances and personnel in 1945. . . . In all these years, women have been very instrumental in all the efforts put forth in work in Congo. Usually women missionaries have outnumbered the men on the field. In spite of this, we have sent out only men when delegations have gone to the field to study, to fellowship and to counsel. At present there are 52 women and 36 men on the list of missionaries in Congo. In a way, it is sad that we have

waited this long to look at the situation as it really is. The call for a women's delegation came from the field itself. We are responding, and excitement is running high both at home and in Congo. [16]

Mary Harder, Canadian WMA president, and Tina Block, a member of the Commission on Overseas Mission (COM) staff, were selected to represent the WMA. Mary would report later that "it was one of the highlights of my life." [17] That it was equally satisfying to the women of Congo was also apparent. The president of the Mennonite Women at Kikwit offered a welcome address to the women. She said: "We have the greatest joy because we can see you with our eyes. Always before we have only seen delegations of men and never women. We used to send you greetings with the men's delegations, but we never knew for sure if you received them or not. This is an affair to marvel at in the history of the women of the Mennonite Church in Congo because the delegation of women from North America has come to visit the women of Congo. Thank you very much and may God be praised in this matter." [18]

The delegates were especially impressed by the lively welcome they received at each stop.

The greetings by the Congolese women were unique. The first greeting was unexpected on our part. We stepped off the plane, got our baggage, went around the building, and there stood about 100 Congolese women and missionaries with five bouquets of flowers singing joyful welcome songs. Tears were fought back as each one of us received the flowers. They greeted us through an interpreter, and we exchanged our greetings. Every station greeted us in a similar way, and yet there was something unique about each welcome. Huge crowds of women, usually the Congolese pastors, and perhaps a few other men, numerous children and missionaries were there. They seemed to come from all directions, all wanting to shake hands. We shook more hands during these three-and-one-half weeks than we did throughout our whole life. Large signs of welcome in both the English and French languages were carried. Sometimes we were asked to walk ahead of the sign and at other times behind it. At a number of stations we received bouquets of flowers. We walked from the airstrip to a church or mission or pastor's home with locked arms, singing Congolese songs. [19]

Women in Mission's COM member would report later that this visit to Zaire elevated the status of the women of Zaire in the eyes of the men of Zaire. [20]

Of the material aid contributions to Zaire through the years, the sewing of layettes was the most ambitious. In the year after WMA became an auxiliary member, 340 layettes were sent to Congo, and the number increased annually. Even as the project began, the officers knew that the baby's garments were not being worn as the contributor probably envisioned, but the value lay in being able to give a gift to the new mother. This was originally designed to bring women into the hospitals to have their babies rather than in unclean conditions in the bush, but the program continued long after that incentive was necessary. At its height, 15,000 layettes were assigned and shipped to Africa. Opposition to the project became increasingly strong, and with the ever-rising duty costs, the growing feeling of independence of Africans, and some internal problems, the layette program was discontinued in 1979. In that year 66 percent of the auxiliary budget was allotted to women's seminars and education for women and girls, a worthwhile emphasis for the times. Only a few hospital supplies were sewed.

When the auxiliary decided in 1972 that the time had come for them to have a representative on the board, and permission was granted, Tina Block of the General Conference became the first woman to serve. She was succeeded by Naomi Lehman, WM president, each serving three years. Before Naomi's appointment, the Commission on Overseas Mission had also appointed its first woman representative. Thus the first three women on the board were from the General Conference.

Since Women in Mission had continued to provide support

for both auxiliary and conference budgeting through the years in which they were part of that organization, they felt entitled to a position on the board comparable to their involvement in General Conference commissions. The coordinator sent a letter of request to the executive secretary of Africa Inter-Mennonite Mission (AIMM) on April 6, 1979, which read in part:

In the course of the last several years, our women's groups have struggled with the whole area of material aid. Also, as mission strategies change, we are wondering how we as an organization can be of most benefit in present mission efforts.

Specifically, in reference to AIMM, there has been a feeling that WM would really appreciate being more directly informed as to what is happening in our mission program in Africa. In view of the fact that AIMM is expanding its work to include not only Zaire, but also Lesotho, Upper Volta and Botswana, and the fact that General Conference, including Women in Mission, is involved with personnel and finances, we would like to request representation from WM on the AIMM board. . . .

In our General Conference structure, WM has had full voting representation on each of our commissions in our Conference. We have found this relationship to be very beneficial to the women as well as to the commissions.[21]

The request was denied.

In support of Women in Mission, the Commission on Overseas Mission continued the search for a way to incorporate a representative of that organization on the AIMM Board. In September 1979, COM recommended that instead of its commission appointing six members to represent the General Conference, Women in Mission could be permitted to assume one of those six positions. The AIMM Board agreed to that arrangement. Jeanne Zook, who was then on the AIMM Board, was named WM representative as well. In essence, the AIMM Board had not changed its original stance, but through the cooperation of COM, which had long recognized the women as strong allies in mission support, Women in Mission did become an official part of the AIMM board.

Young Mission Workers

A natural extension of the Women's Missionary Association was its auxiliary for children. No one knew better than mothers that early training was essential for performance in any given area, and interest in missions should be developed in childhood; but this promotion was one which never reached the goals set for it.

By official resolution in 1933 it was agreed "that the executive committee be empowered to appoint a secretary of Junior and Intermediate Girls societies who shall in cooperation with the officers and committees of the association, try to further missionary interest in this department of work." [22] Mrs. J. Ernest Cline of Upland, California, was appointed secretary and a page in *Missionary News and Notes* was given for the promotion of the work.

As the program progressed, each district was encouraged to set up its own junior program. By 1945 five districts had appointed junior-intermediate secretaries, with the chairperson appointed by the WMA. Even as the program was organized, the officers said children were already involved in so many things that an added activity was really not appropriate. Martha Goerz wrote to the junior chairperson, "When I became editor I felt that *News and Notes* could and should become the avenue through which we might reach our children as well as women. It has always been my belief that in order to have mission-minded men and women it is best to interest them in the tender years of childhood. I therefore suggested to our committee that we start a separate department for the children.... But we soon found just as you wrote that children also now have more societies and activities than they have time for and that we would have to depend on existing groups mostly at least." [23]

They chose to work through Sunday school classes and evening programs, although some churches did establish *mission bands.* The First Mennonite Church of Berne, Indiana, for instance, continued with active mission bands until 1977. One of the problems was that in the United States the program never clearly defined what ages were included in the groups. Some churches reported everyone from three years old through high school, but program helps were hard to produce for that wide a range.

For some groups the department was patterned after their women's group, with similar fund-raising projects. The March 1935 issue of *Missionary News and Notes* reported, "Girls, like their mothers, earned money by cents . . . selling baked things. . . . Mother would bake and I would sell . . . made potholders . . . picked cherries and sold them. . . . Mother made tiebacks and stuffed hangers which I sold . . . baked cakes . . . made my money by selling butter and cream . . . sold chickens and eggs . . . helped my aunt can fruit and ran errands for her . . . sold coffee cakes . . . picked chickens . . . buying flower seeds and selling them for 5¢ . . . making angel food cakes for 25¢ and selling them for 50¢." [24]

Junior-intermediates became *Young Mission Workers* in 1953 as leaders tried to broaden the program. One chairperson made an appeal to missionaries to write literature especially designed to acquaint children with conference mission work. Each child was to contribute four cents for this project.

A *Leader's Resource Manual for Young Mission Workers* appeared in 1965. It was an excellent guide prepared by the WMA Literature Committee and was intended to be used as supplemental help for *The Christian Mission of the General Conference Mennonite Church* by Dr. S. F. Pannabecker. After the introductory pages which described the functions of the organization, it began:

> Because history lessons can very easily disintegrate into an uninteresting recital of facts, names and dates, the following stories are included to show children that *people* make history. People and God make the history of the Christian Church of which Mennonites are a part. [25]

The manual was the only one of its kind published for juniors, but smaller project and program books offered excellent helps to leaders.

Canada fared much better, with boys and girls actively involved in Wayfarers, Pioneer Girls, and Torchbearer programs. Some of these were sponsored by Women in Mission groups, but many were congregation sponsored. Mrs. Helen Janzen was appointed Canadian Junior-Intermediate secretary, and she wrote of the program in Saskatchewan in 1968: "The Wayfarer's Club of the Mennonite church is a personal achievement program for girls from the ages of nine to fourteen. . . . Saskatchewan is the only province that has a province-wide organized girls' club with a conference being held each year. . . . (We) use the Program and Project Ideas booklet for Young Mission Workers." [26] Many women's mission societies continue to sponsor clubs for boys and girls today.

The peak year for Young Mission Workers in the United States was 1968 when there were 164 reporting groups with a membership of 4,136 boys and girls. In spite of qualified, capable leadership, the program began to decline, and by 1979 only nineteen groups were reporting. The Eastern District ceased sponsorship of the program, and discouragement was felt in other districts as well.

The Women in Mission Council recommended in 1977 that Young Mission Worker sponsors continue to be considered as resource persons for their district and to be elected or appointed there, but that the Women in Mission coordinator be the advisory chairperson. It was also decided that once a triennium all sponsors should attend Council of Commissions meetings to become acquainted with their co-workers. The WM office lent assistance by providing special goals and projects for juniors. At General Conference central offices all funds identified as coming from children's groups were turned over to Women in Mission for record keeping, but most of the contributing groups were functioning without guidance by WM.

The Western District sponsor wrote, "Possibly one of the reasons children and young people rebel against the church and often leave at an early age is because they do not feel that they are a part of the church, its life and work. If this is so, we as adults need to provide opportunities for children to be active in our churches—to find creative outlets for their interest and energy." [27] But the duplication of efforts for Sunday schools, vacation Bible schools, and evening groups did not solve the problem.

6 winds of change

In the late 1960s a movement in the secular world for women's liberation was making itself felt. Feared, applauded, hated, or supported, it was to make its mark on the church world as well. At the General Assembly of the National Council of Churches in December of 1969, a women's caucus met. There were women delegates at that council, but none of them had been given anything more than a superficial part in the proceedings. In tones much more moderate than the calls of secular liberation, they made an appeal to the council to be an accepted part of the total program. Later a United Methodist woman who was part of that movement reported as follows:

> Three years ago, in December of 1969, I stood before the General Assembly of the NCCUSA as the designated voice of the Women's Caucus. The statement of that Caucus was one of the first examples of a new consciousness and sense of solidarity among women in the church.... At that time we stated that we had just begun to find a coherent voice and to organize ourselves. We were not too proud to say that we were not too well organized at that Assembly. Even

now, we force ourselves to speak what we really feel. In one way, it would be so much easier to leave you alone to go on about your business - if it were your business, but it's *our Lord's business*, and because we still hold onto the belief that it may be so, we must participate. [1]

At that assembly the women involved were divided in their thinking about the women's missionary associations which were part of every denomination. Some thought the time had come for all separate organizations, both male and female, to be done away with. Others felt that women's organizations ought to be one means of helping all women achieve a greater church involvement, including those who were not members of their group. For the WMA, new vigor and drive resulted when they followed the latter route.

In the Mennonite church it was another four years before there would be concerted action to involve more women at General Conference level. In October 1973 there was a consultation on the role of women in the church held at Mennonite Biblical Seminary. The vice-presidents of the Women's Missionary Association were in part instrumental in promoting and calling for the consultation which opened doors not only for the organization but more importantly for both women and men of the entire conference. Leaders from each of the commissions, the seminary, WMA, and some at large were chosen for the intense discussions. Frustration, joy, and hope marked the responses to the sessions, and an opening wedge was made in conference relationships.

Perhaps the most significant result of this for Women in Mission was not its promotion, but that it drew the organization into the mainstream of the conference and demanded of it cooperation and closer ties with the commissions. It also brought to the commissions a new awareness of the strengths and vitality of the ten thousand women who were involved in its structure.

Three of the recommendations made to the WMA at that consultation were to have far-reaching effects. The easiest to implement was to change the name of the association to a more accurate description of today's women. *Women in Mission*, claiming every woman to have a mission in the church, became the official name at the next triennial session in St. Catherines, Ontario, in 1974. The name met with instant acceptance. Every province and district changed the title of its larger organization to *Women in Mission*, with the Western District the last to do so.

A second recommendation made to the WMA at that consultation was that the women's association, Commission on Education (COE), and Commission on Home Ministries (CHM) were to hire a staff person for three years to work on the issue of "women in the church." Herta Funk was subsequently hired for part-time work on this issue, with WM agreeing to pay part of her salary.

The third recommendation was that which called for the General Board of the conference to allow WM to be represented on each commission by one voting member. Long years before, in the 1920s, missionaries had written the WMA executives that women ought to be on the Foreign Mission Board instead of on the sidelines, but the suggestion was obviously too radical to consider. By 1972 the pull for greater participation was strong enough that Doris Weber, secretary of WMA, was instructed to write to the General Board asking that two members of the WMA be allowed to become representatives on the commissions. This was granted by the board except that the representation was "unofficial" because of constitutional limitations. The women appointed became interested and active on the commissions, but they were not allowed to vote. The one exception was the Commission on Home Ministries which appointed them to committees and asked them to function in the same manner as other commission members. By the end of 1972, all the commissions had recorded in their minutes the desire for such continuing representation.

At the suggestion of the conference general secretary, Weber wrote another letter to the General Board requesting that the official status of this membership be reviewed and

Women in Mission Executive Committee and Staff - 1980

confirmed. The board referred this matter to the Constitution Committee of the conference for further action.[2] After considerable delay, the Constitution Committee recommended the following:

- —agreed to recommend to the Nominating Committee that women should be on the General Conference ballot in greater numbers than previously.
- —agreed to recommend that the General Board urge the WMA to continue to appoint representatives to the commissions without vote, for discussion and participation according to previous practice.[3]

The Executive Committee of the WMA, showing distinct signs of being tired of getting pushed around, "indicated that through the past months their feeling has definitely changed from a passive stance of not 'demanding but accepting the appointments' to a strong indication that *a change of some kind is a must if the WMA is to relate meaningfully.*"[4]

When the Constitution Committee made its final report denying them voting privileges because they were "a special interest group," matters came to a head. Although the overseas mission and education commissions dropped the WMA representatives from their boards, the Commission on Home Ministries ignored the opinion and continued to involve the two WMA representatives actively, as Martha Nickel reported, "The on again, off again appointments to the commissions haven't really affected us. CHM has always considered us *on*."[5]

Stung by the "special interest group" label, convinced they had rightful causes for representation, and supported by the commission executive secretaries, Women in Mission coordinator Gladys Goering, representing the women's group, appeared before the General Board with a statement which read in part:

> We feel our Association should be entitled to representation for the following reasons:
> 1. We are the voice of 10,692 women who belong to WMA. Since 2/5 of us are Canadian, we have a kind of bond which helps unite the General Conference.
> 2. The giving of money and material aid by women's groups to the conference, the district, the province, and communities has in the past four years run well over a half million dollars annually. MCC is receiving an ever increasing share; we feel it is past time that the General Conference recognize also the tremendous potential of our group by giving us voting positions on the Commissions.
> 3. To be part of the Commissions would mean for us to learn more about our conference, to be more informed about its total program, and therefore more equipped to communicate this. We are anything but "a special interest group," as described by the constitutional committee. We have been contributing to conference work ever since our origin.
> 4. We realize that ideally there should be a much greater percentage of women on the commissions, but we know that in all probability this will be a long time in coming. We suggest, therefore, that placing one of our leaders - a member of the executive council - as a voting member on

each of the commissions would be an asset to you as well as to us.

5. Our WMA is currently reassessing our place in the church, and our future direction. To be a working part of the commissions could be of real help to us. To be shut out will say something to us also."[6]

WMA recommended that the representation be tried on a three-year basis with a reevaluation at that time, although they were convinced of the capabilities of the women they would appoint.

The General Board granted the request by unanimous vote. Later, similar representation on the Seminary Board was also granted and the bylaws amended accordingly. Three years later the representation was extended "until further notice."[7]

The first four women named to be official representatives were: Margaret Ewert, Canadian WM president, Commission on Overseas Mission; Martha Nickel, WM vice-president, Commission on Home Ministries; Lora Oyer, WM vice-president, Commission on Education; and Helen Kruger, WM Literature Committee member, Mennonite Biblical Seminary Board. They were the forerunners of other capable individuals subsequently appointed.

With a new name, a new official conference relationship, and a new publication, *Window to Mission*, came the desire for another new feature, an emblem representative of all women in mission. A contest was held to find a logo which would picture this association of women, eager to be part of the church in old and new ways. From the entries received, the one chosen was the work of a twenty-one-year-old art student. Cindy Stucky described her design in these words: "The dove symbolizes woman's desire for peace and our efforts to achieve it. The separation of the cross and circle (in the biological symbol for woman) pictures our new liberation from old bonds—a freedom to make use of our individual abilities. The circular portion of the symbol for woman encircling the globe is woman's encompassing love and concern for people. In the center of all is the cross representing God's guidance in our lives and work."[8] The attractive stationery now bore the emblem, the names of officers and staff, and the simple heading *Women in Mission*. How much more inclusive that was than the first official stationery in 1918 which was printed "Executive Committee of the Sewing Societies."

In 1970 Betty Epp, who was then president of WMA, was the first woman elected to serve on the MCC Board. During her term she was the *only* woman to sit on the council. After her time expired, the WMA appointed Lora Oyer to succeed her as a member of the MCC Peace Section, at its invitation. Lora found her specific field of interest in the young women struggling to be accepted in the work of the total church. She wrote in her report to the WM Council, "We can't write off this group of dedicated, concerned young mothers and singles who want to relate to other Christian women, who want opportunities to be involved and to be a more integral part of the total church."[9]

Her concerns helped bring WM into closer understanding of their problems. The first grants-in-aid allotted to Mennonite Biblical Seminary students were in 1968, and the amounts increased in coming years; but personal contacts with seminary students and graduates came more slowly.

When Naomi Wollmann succeeded Lora on the Peace Section, the area which appealed to her and which she helped develop was the influence of television as it related to violence, physical and emotional. A brochure which she wrote entitled "What Is Television Teaching Your Family" was published by WM and CHM and distributed to over nine thousand readers. Her appointment to the Commission on Home Ministries' Committee on Media continued to draw Women in Mission into closer ties with missions at home, and called on them to be alert to the good and bad of the television industry. Another tie with the commission came in the appointment of a WM representative to the Peace and

Social Concerns Committee of CHM. Also in the seventies, when the Commission on Education called for sewing skills once more, women made one thousand hand puppets to be introduced with the new Foundation Series Sunday school materials.

New Relationships

A new venture internationally was the cooperation of Women in Mission with women in India. When the first All India Mennonite Women's Conference was in its planning stages, P. J. Malagar of Dhamtari wrote to the Commission on Overseas Mission asking if it would be willing to lend support to this important first, and the commission turned the letter over to Women in Mission. At its annual council session in February 1977, Women in Mission responded with enthusiasm. They sent a cablegram to Malagar which read: "General Conference Women in Mission encourage All India Mennonite Women's Conference. Plan to send participants and support. Details incomplete." [10]

Women in Mission's two vice-presidents, Lois Deckert of Kansas and Martha Nickel of Saskatchewan, were chosen to be their representatives. As they were about to leave for India eight months later, coordinator Joan Wiebe wrote to the council,

> We are getting ready to put our two representatives, Martha Nickel and Lois Deckert on the plane. We're excited with them! Together with over 200 women from India, they, and eight other "overseas women" will be meeting from November 1-6 using as their theme, 'We are one in Christ.' They will be sharing, singing, listening, studying, eating and drinking tea together. Martha will be leading a Bible Study on Ephesians 1 and 2 and Lois will be sharing about WM and its various phases of outreach and activities. They will also be doing some traveling to various regions, meeting our Indian sisters. [11]

On their return both women traveled extensively in the United States and Canada, relating experiences to interested women at home who had helped make them possible. Lois, for whom the trip had been a return to the land in which she had grown up as a daughter of missionaries, told the council:

What an experience WM made possible for Martha and myself! . . . There were 210 women gathered as delegates, guests and observers at this conference. They came from Andhra Pradesh (South India), Madhya Pradesh (Central India), Bihar and Calcutta. They represented the MB, BC, MC, Brethren in Christ, and United Missionary churches. There were professional women as well as those of us who are homemakers. Some had facility in several languages, others were not so fortunate. There were young women and old women, serious and humorous women, white, light brown and dark brown women. Some women came from generations of Christians and others were newer Christians. This was a real mix where the Spirit could work and where unity in Christ was experienced in a warm and tangible way. . . . We left India with our minds so full of experiences, both new, and for me, renewed that it has taken a good while to sort through them. [12]

Martha Nickel's report was equally enthusiastic.

God still allows miracles to happen even in our world today. The conference itself was a miracle - a definite answer to many prayers. The fact that Lois and I could attend was a miracle - also an answer to many prayers. . . . From the time we arrived in India we sensed the excitement and anticipation felt by the women for the conference which was only about three weeks away. Many had saved their paisas (pennies) for months so that donations could be made for conference expenses. To be chosen a delegate was a new experience for many. For some village women this would be the first time away from home, the first train ride and many other first time experiences. Some of the women were quite apprehensive. How would their families get along without them? Would they be able to understand all that happened at a conference? It was a very difficult decision to make. Leah Sonwani[13] took us to a number of homes where some more encouragement was needed before a decision could be

96

made. It was the "Leah's" who put their heart and soul into conference planning that made the conference a reality. [14]

It remained for Leah herself to summarize the real worth of the experience in a letter to Women in Mission following the conference. She wrote, "I want to thank you for sending Martha and Lois to us. Their visit here was very inspiring to the people. In a way we are developing more understanding and love towards our friends from overseas." [15]

The experience of hosting the Taiwan choir in 1978 was another rewarding international undertaking. The tour was arranged to include a week at Mennonite World Conference in Kansas, the motivating factor for the Taiwanese. A missionary in Taiwan, Martha Vandenberg, saw an added value if North American women could be involved in the tour plans. She wrote to General Conference WM Vice-President Mary Anne Boschman, "Personally I feel this type of exchange would be of great benefit to WM as well as for our ladies. It can also help our countries in understanding each other and appreciating each other." [16] Twenty-four women, representing three generations, gave concerts in five provinces and eight states where they made more than thirty

Taiwan Mennonite Women's Choir

appearances. Women in Mission made all travel and concert arrangements. Except for a few meals on the road, Women in Mission provided lodging, food, and transportation for the month's itinerary. The choir members were introduced to "carry-in dinners," American and Canadian menus, and numerous stops with Mennonite families in their homes. "Through the women's visit, God has done a new and beautiful thing among us in that we have been able to see Taiwan and some of its people through new lenses. What a great gift they gave us by sharing their lives with us through their songs of faith, their radiant smiles and gracious manner," wrote the WM coordinator. [17]

A letter from the choir after their return to Taiwan was equally warm: "We are rested from the physical tiredness and are left with a real feeling of joy, thanksgiving and wonder at the beauty of the 'body of Christ' which transcends language, cultural and ethnic barriers. We have travelled many miles, eaten unfamiliar foods, heard different languages and appreciated the changing panorama of Canada and the United States of America. We are impressed with the vastness of your country and the hospitality of your people." [18]

As another part of their involvement in Mennonite World Conference, Women in Mission contributed toward grants given to fifteen overseas women, which enabled them to attend conference. Women in Mission also accepted further responsibilities in planning for and assisting with women's sharing times and an international banquet. A committee specially appointed for this assignment included representatives from four different Mennonite women's groups and the MCC Task Force on Women.

A program encouraging international exchanges has been part of the budget since 1974. WM helps underwrite the costs of enabling wives of overseas pastors studying at Mennonite Biblical Seminary to come to America with them. The women who come to this country are frequently invited by local or district women's groups to share time with them and to become acquainted with each other. The emphasis on relating to women from overseas is, of course, not new. But again, the days which encouraged more travel and personal contact than had been possible before also brought increased appreciation of the worth of meeting personally. The Executive Committee of WM in 1979 set as their goals, relevant to women overseas, "Enrichment of women in developing countries" through scholarships and school training, helping prepare women for leadership in their own country, understanding the role of women and their needs, and the desire to relate to and share with each other around the world.[19] Included in WM's budget was "Women's World Outreach," which was set up to provide education and professional training.

In February 1978 the WM Advisory Council received a letter from a female seminarian asking for guidelines for women in church vocations and asking how she could relate in special ways to women and others that men cannot. A meeting was called at Council of Commissions to be devoted to women in church vocations, and several professional women met with Women in Mission. Helpful and sympathetic exchanges of visions, fears, and frustrations drew them closer together. When goals for the next decade were set, Women in Mission saw the need for themselves to "be a supportive group.... Affirm those happy with the status quo. . . . To those exercising newfound gifts and trying their wings, together presenting our gift to God."[20]

In their relationships to all women they saw as a first step the need for personal strengthening and spiritual growth. Gift discernment for themselves and assisting others to find their gifts was high priority. They called for ways to deal with the breakdown of family traditions and morals. They were, in effect, calling for a mission to themselves, an appeal to equip themselves and their families with greater skills needed to cope with the pressures of the day. The ability to say what they felt, to record what they felt, came with the times; the women of 1917 could not have felt free to set these goals, perhaps not even to think them.

The drama of women seeking a place in the mission of the church in the 1970s holds striking comparisons with those in the beginning years of the mission organization. In both time spans, the work of women in support of the church went on without interruption while the leaders struggled for recognition for the group. In both times there was tremendous energy and ability to be tapped, which was being offered to the church. In both times, opposition and lukewarm support almost meant the end of the involvement, but the need of women to be active promoters in the work of the church was stronger.

The search continues.

7 the home front

We joined hands to be workers together in the building of God's kingdom and in spreading the Gospel of Jesus Christ... knotted comforters for relief... rolled bandages.. . quilted to increase our mission giving ... had missionary prayer partners . . . served sales and banquets . . . remembered wedding anniversaries ... tended to needs in church kitchen ... heard guest speakers ... visited sick, shut-ins, and the lonely ... purchased books and placed in church library ... helped at Relief Center ... volunteered time at MCC self help shops... donated to MCC relief sales ... supported college ... donated food ... helped with day care center . . . filled district and General Conference assignments . . . were in charge of (church) showers for newlyweds ... held mother-daughter banquets... provided flowers . . . remembered missionaries with gifts and prayers . . . furnished rooms in hospitals and homes . . . sewed for needy families in community... canned for relief ... made Christmas bundles, layette bundles, leper bundles . . . gave blankets, thousands of quilt blocks . . . held mission sales, bazaars ... bought piano for the church ... heard spiritual and inspirational messages ... had public programs on missions ... did extensive study of missions..

. raised money . . . contributed to church improvement fund . . . fostered good singing . . . bought hymnaries . . . sewed . . . pieced quilts . . . worked with juniors . . . made stuffed animals . . . equipped parsonage. . . . [1]

This resumé of an active mission group in Kansas could be repeated with some variations by many others in Canada and the United States, and no history of General Conference women is complete without a look at the local, district, and provincial organizations.

Much of the initial organization of local women's groups came about through the help and involvement of men. One of the earliest societies was formed in 1881 at the Hereford Church in Bally, Pennsylvania. When Rev. C. H. van der Smissen spoke to the women in 1938, he proudly told them that he was the founder of their group over fifty years earlier. [2] The entire van der Smissen family was known to promote missions, with Sister Hillegonda given credit for writing the first history of women's mission organizations in the General Conference. [3]

To Middle District also goes the credit for a directive to the ministers in 1888 to see that regular mission sermons were preached, and that mission societies were founded. [4] This executive approval undoubtedly helped women's groups organize, and by 1900 the conference report would show that there was a women's mission society in every church in the conference.

The Berne, Indiana, *Nähverein* ("sewing society") was started in 1887 at the suggestion of the pastor. He presided at the first meeting and continued to attend each meeting of the young organization. [5]

In many groups the meeting could not start until the minister came to have opening prayer. This was true not only in the beginning years but a long time after. It was not so much what men could do as opposed to what women could do, but what was proper for a lay person and what required a pastor's skills. The repeated requests for prayer support in women's publications obviously had no reference to being able to lead out in prayer in a group. In one Washington church where the pastor had to open the afternoon meeting with prayer, it was customary that he and his wife be invited out to dinner before the meeting. In a Kansas congregation, the pastor called the women together in 1894 to organize a sisters' sewing society. He conducted the first election, in which two of his daughters became officers, drew up a constitution for the society, and continued to preside at their annual business meetings, as did his successor.[6] The practice was discontinued when the minister's wife was elected president.

A South Dakota mission society solved the problem of needing to have a man's help by placing both the pastors' wives and the pastors on a committee to draw up the constitution for them.[7] Early sample constitutions sent to newly organizing societies suggested that men could be considered honorary members. The Zion Church of Souderton, Pennsylvania, went along with that suggestion, asking that honorary members pay the same fifty cents annual dues as the women. The Bethany Church of Quakertown, Pennsylvania, apparently provided a better bargain, as they list "Honorary memberships given to 8 men."

That the Western District Women's Organization was given a position on the district Executive Council was due to the district minister, Elbert Koontz, who was personally instrumental in first inviting their president to become part of the council.

But the history of women's groups is not an account of the men who functioned as promoters and aides, welcome and valuable as they were. It is the story of lay persons and societies which began their history in homes, for the most part, where many still continue. In one Kansas congregation, for example, the women celebrated the twenty-fifth anniversary of their founding in the same home in which it began.[8] It was in their homes that women felt a freedom to be themselves and to use their abilities. Sometimes a woman would invite several friends to her house for fellowship and refreshments to discuss the possibility of meeting regularly. Often a missionary in the area would be present to promote the cooperation of missionary and the supporting groups.

Organization was usually informal, and most met for several years before framing a constitution. Small children came along with their mothers and often played and sang beneath the canopy of the quilt. One little boy who sat under the quilt and listened to the missionary stories which Sister Hillegonda read to the women as they stitched grew up to be a missionary to Congo; his name was Waldo Harder.[9] A Washingtonian recalls that, as little boys, he and his brother had to model clothing his mother made when she was on the cutting committee; he remembers them being of muslin, undoubtedly sewn for a boy his size in India.[10] Another little boy cried when he grew old enough to go to school and had to miss mother's mission society meetings. A mother in one congregation used to long for the day when there would be more adults than children present. Although some groups deliberately refrained from serving refreshments when they met only half days, many enjoyed "vaspa" (afternoon lunch) before leaving for home. Where women met for the whole day, a meal was necessary, and the friendly exchanges were a pleasant part of mission society day. In earlier times some women seem to have been able to handle horse and buggy to come to meeting themselves, but others needed their husbands to escort them to the meeting place. Sometimes the men spent the same hours at mission society as the women, enjoying each other's company in an adjoining room. In Indiana women walked to mission society in town, carrying their babies, rather than miss a meeting. Several Canadian groups tell about coming to meeting in sleighs, even when it was forty degrees below zero! In Superb, Saskatchewan, the pastor was on hand to give haircuts to the men who had chauffeured their wives to mission society, and, as an extra bonus, the fifty-cent charge was given to the society.[11]

When the groups became too large to meet in homes, and churches were built with extra rooms, many of the societies began to gather at the church. Even meeting at church did not mean using the sanctuary. Quite the contrary, basements, furnished and unfurnished, became the women's headquarters. One Idaho group met in a section of the church basement which was not finished and had a dirt floor. The furnace was in the middle of the basement and behind it was a three-burner kerosine stove which they used to heat coffee, served in cups they had brought from home.[12] From Ohio comes a similar account of women who met in the partially excavated part of the church basement and quilted all day while the coffeepot simmered away on the old potbellied stove.[13]

In a Kansas congregation the women met in the church dining house which was located in the corner of the churchyard some distance away.[14] In another, women met at the church only for the annual business meeting, which was always conducted by the pastor.[15] It seems obvious that women did not consider their sphere of church work on a par with worship and church school, nor did they feel it proper or comfortable to meet where worship services were held.

Today, many churches have well-equipped mission society rooms which are attractive and convenient. In some congregations there is a movement back to meeting in homes for a more personal feeling, the "small group" experience. In others, the convenience of a church is being discovered by groups which previously met in homes. Many of the larger groups divide into smaller units, feeling it is more meaningful, but at Berne, Indiana, between two and three hundred women meet together regularly for their monthly sessions. At the other end of the spectrum are societies with only five members, and some Canadian groups record that they began with three members. There are no rules for either size or method of functioning.

Not all groups sewed. The term "our mission and sewing societies" in the first year indicated a difference of approach. The treasurer had ordered their first stationery using "Sewing Societies" in the heading, but when it was time to reorder, Susannah Haury advised, "I do hope you had 'Missionary Societies of General Conf. of Menn. instead of Sewing Societies.' I think the latter is a misnomer, because of the societies which *do not sew*, but they are all 'Missionary Societies,' even if they don't."[16] A mission society of 1917 would have been surprised at the variety of subjects discussed by a Toronto group fifty years later as they studied marriage, child bearing, old age, pollution, natural foods, mental retardation, the status of Indians in Toronto, and prisoner rehabilitation. Although a majority of the mission groups had sewing projects through the years, many did not, and there appears to have been mild tension among them as to which form of mission society was more needed.

As sewing assignments from the conference decreased sharply in the 1970s, Mennonite Central Committee relief sales have offered increased opportunities to use sewing skills. MCC's self-help shops also lean away from sewing to be done by local women in favor of supporting overseas persons to increase their own productivity and market. In 1962 the WMA adviser chairperson cautioned, "As the mission work shifts from dependent churches to the indigenous so must our work change to keep in step with progress."[17] In some ways this has been difficult for North American women to accept. "They don't want what we can do," a woman at a Western District workshop was overheard to say. The shift in direction is inevitable. The association of local mission groups with Mennonite Central Committee has always been a strong factor, and with the increasing number of relief sales, self-help and thrift shops, there is great demand for the cooperation of many women who find satisfaction in these commitments.

Congregations have been the recipients of church equipment provided by the local women's society. Kitchens were often outfitted by societies, as were nurseries. Many library books and Sunday school supplies, especially for children, have been given. One group bought dining tables, another purchased a pulpit Bible, while another contributed altar cloths and Communion linens. Several groups bought a piano for the church. Carpeting was given. A suit for the minister was listed on several reports, one "very formal - it had tails," which the minister modeled for the ladies.[18] The women's organization of the Germantown Mennonite Church, the first Mennonite church in the United States, began in order to set up a fund for repairs badly needed for its restoration. A Canadian group raised money to buy two acres of land for a church site.[19] Curtains and drapes, pulpits, hymnals, choir robes, a mimeograph machine for the youth group, church pews, record players, velvet offering bags—the list of donations is endless.

Of significance in the history of women's organizations is their support of area colleges and schools. From the opening of Wadsworth Seminary through the years in which Mennonite colleges and Bible and parochial schools flourished, the steady support in money contributions from women can be counted, but the greater contributions of service and moral support cannot be tabulated. Scholarship funds for both local and international students have been provided, as have countless incidents of hospitality. The first project adopted by Manitoba and Saskatchewan women was the Margareta Toews Scholarship Fund for students at the academy in Gretna, a continuing project. Freeman Junior College is included in the district women's annual budget, and the spring *Schmeckfest* at the college demands hours of labor before, after, and during the occasion. The Central District Women in Mission includes Bluffton College in its annual giving, especially including funds for international students. Bethel College's Fall Festival utilizes the time and talents of hundreds of women each year, and both Pacific and Western District women support the college financially. Every provincial WM organization includes Canadian Mennonite Bible College in its giving. Area Bible colleges and schools in each province and many states rely on the labors and giving of women's groups. Mennonite Biblical Seminary, the only school included in the General Conference Women in Mission budget, holds a special place in local group interest and support. In addition to budget, women have contributed furnishings for missionary apartments and student quarters, as well as scholarships.

Two great strengths of the local societies are seen in service and fellowship. Within the congregation and community, women's groups are depended on to provide services at funerals, weddings, and gatherings of various kinds. Catering meals is on the list of numerous societies as a function performed when it is convenient and often when it is not. Churches and homes for the aged as well as area schools benefit from cleanup days sponsored by women. Retreat grounds and buildings have equipment given by women, and many women fill the necessary jobs during summer retreats. Help is provided for bloodmobiles and Red Cross functions. Many societies serve as hostesses when choirs or other groups are church guests. When people are hospitalized it is often the mission group which provides assistance to the family during the hospitalization and to the patient on her return home. Day-care centers rely heavily on donated labor, as do church-sponsored nursery schools. "In homes where sickness or death has entered, the members of the society in an organized way will help bear burdens," records an early history of Northern District. [20] The key word is "organized," which adds a plus to the service and assures those in need of assistance that someone is equipped to be of immediate help. MCC's shops could not exist without the hours of labor given without charge. Nor could one count the hours spent by society members visiting with and listening to shut-ins and lonely people as part of their regular outreach.

The fellowship provided for women as the mission societies came into being was an obvious highlight for them, as it still is. Some groups keep the same basic membership for years, and friendship is strengthened. An Ontario group said, "Though we are not a large group, around twenty-five members, we are closely drawn to one another, thereby experiencing very meaningful fellowship with one another."[21] One Manitoba society declared, "Our years together have been marked by warm times of fellowship, prayer, growing, and maturing as Christians. We have shared joys and sorrows in friendship, grief, sickness, and death. This has united us, strengthened our faith in God, the church and each other."[22]

A criticism leveled at the local group is that the close-knit group sometimes becomes a closed group, and anyone not included feels shut out and unnecessary. Some of the larger groups have taken the approach of changing membership in individual circles regularly in order to enable women to meet and associate with a larger number of members in the congregation. This allows for more intergenerational experience, which in small congregations happens of necessity. In both instances it is considered a plus.

No program of the General Conference can function without the support of the local constituents, and Women in Mission has grown on the loyalty and response of local societies.

In District and Conference

Women of each area first began to get a regional "feel" by joining together to give programs at conference time. The first to do so were the women of Central District, who include in their history being part of Middle District and Central Conference. Since this was also the area in which the General Conference came into being, this is not surprising. Their first program given for the societies only was in 1889. It was attended by "many friends, brothers and sisters." It was not until 1891 that an advance notice was given in *Bundesbote* that, God willing, there would be a meeting of the Sewing Societies in Berne, Indiana, the day after the close of the conference. The reception must have been favorable, because at the next conference the women were given a time *during* the conference to present their program to the entire gathering. The *Bundesbote* reported that the program "was well attended, the presentations of the sisters being well thought out, practical, and constructive, also read loudly enough that one could understand them. A number of preachers spoke at the close very encouragingly to the sisters."[23]

Spurred on by their success, the women of the Middle District decided they would give a program at the next General Conference sessions which were being hosted in their district at Pandora, Ohio. That program given in 1893 was a first for the women; and although it would be another twenty-four years before they would become an official women's missionary association in the General Conference, they would continue to be responsible for an evening's missionary program through 1959.

Central Conference women became a district conference organization in 1925 under the name of "Conference Ladies Aid Society." They were an original part of the Congo Inland Mission Auxiliary described earlier, and leaders in that work. In the early 1940s the conference started calling for a brief report of the women's activities, and in 1945 they were given an afternoon to present their program and conduct their business during regular conference hours. Dr. S. F. Pannabecker wrote, "From this time on they were recognized as the Conference Women's Organization."[24] The Central Conference and the Middle District merged officially in 1957 and became the Central District of the General Conference.

The first mention of district activity for Pacific District women is recorded in the minutes of the district in October 1907. They read: "Encourage the women's mission societies of our district to have a yearly meeting in connection with our conference and give them a time to tell us of their work." Obviously the recommendation was heeded and at the session one year later the conference by resolution thanked "the Ladies' Mission Societies for the good program they gave, the individual members, and choir for the good songs they brought."[25] At the time she became president, Susannah Haury belonged to the first society organized in Pacific District in 1903 at Paso Robles, and it was to this group which she turned automatically when she needed extra help. In 1927 the mission societies officially organized as Pacific District Women's Missionary Societies.

One project of special interest to Pacific District Women in Mission has been the Indian school at Oraibi, Arizona, to which they have given substantial gifts.

Distance between mission societies is a factor keeping Pacific District women from getting together frequently. As a result of this the women decided to subdivide into state units in the hopes that more frequent gatherings would be possible. There are western Washington, eastern Washington, Oregon, and California fellowships which meet once a year. As early as 1957 there was an allotment in the district women's budget of twenty-five cents per member for travel costs, which enabled the district adviser to keep in touch with the societies.

In June 1974 the Executive Committee of Pacific District WM approached the Executive Committee of the district with the request that the WM president be included in the district Executive Board as a representative of the women. They were informed that this would be unconstitutional, but that their president could attend, except on special occasions, without voting rights. When the WM officers took the matter to the annual meeting, a motion to seek an amendment to the constitution was lost, and the matter was dropped.

Eastern District women were organized in 1924 and had their first full meeting the next year. Apparently they functioned as an independent unit, and the attempts of the General Conference Executive Committee to have them work more closely with them were not very successful. One of the reasons might have been that the WMA tried to make contacts through the pastors, often without much success. One pastor told them the societies were a leading factor in the district orphanage society, but another pastor said that although the women were organized there wasn't much activity. Susannah Haury hoped that the women would become more General-Conference minded because in their

111

groups they had "a methodical way of working" [26] which she felt could be put to good use in the General Conference. By 1943 the Eastern District held its first mid-year meeting, a practice continued since that time.

While most of the districts and provinces have one meeting in conjunction with the conference's annual business meetings, Eastern District WM schedules theirs independent of the conference. They feel the need for a full day to themselves, and since many of the societies are within a few miles of each other, travel costs are not prohibitive.

Eastern District owns and operates the Frederick Mennonite Home, a facility for the aged, and Women in Mission is very actively involved in services for the home. The kitchen has heavy stainless steel cookware provided by WM, as well as many drapes and slipcovers and other equipment. A special Home Committee is appointed annually by WM. Two other committees which function under WM are the Bluffton College Women's Advisory Council and the Women's Committee for Men-O-Lan Campground. In the early years of the women's society their work and the work of the orphanage society was almost inseparable, and until 1976 the mission societies included a Women's Orphanage Committee. Annie Funk, an early General Conference missionary, came from the first society organized in the Eastern District, at Bally, Pennsylvania, in 1881.

The first mention of Northern District women in the official minutes of the conference is in 1911 where each of the ten churches in the conference lists a *Nähverein* ("sewing society"). Two years later only five of twelve churches had Nähvereins, and four years later there were only three left. There is no mention of women's meetings until 1926 when their officer reported, "Monday evening, June 21, was set aside by the conference program committee for a Sewing Society program. As this was the first time in the history of the district conference, it was looked upon chiefly as an experiment. . . . The program as a whole was very instructive and inspiring and many of the ladies expressed a desire that

112

this might become a permanent part of our conference program."[27] If there was a program the following year, it was not part of the record, but after 1928 the societies are mentioned annually. A full publishing of the program first appeared in 1930, and in 1949 the speeches delivered at the women's program were reprinted in full, as were the other official reports of the entire Northern District. One might assume that the women had arrived. As in other districts, the women's programs always included missionaries, and their appearance on occasion in garb of the country in which they worked left lasting impressions. The first mission society in Northern District was formed in Mt. Lake, Minnesota, in 1885 with Mrs. Abraham Penner, mother of P. A. Penner, as its first president, a post she held for twenty-six years.[28]

There is conflicting information about where the first mission society among General Conference churches in Canada was begun. Mrs. G. A. Krehbiel, first Canadian adviser, reported that in 1907 the first group was formed in Rosthern, Saskatchewan, but in their recent WM Canadian history it was stated that societies existed in Manitoba as early as 1892. The great influx of immigrants beginning in the 1920s resulted in a large increase in the number of women's groups, and the Canadian records show most of their groups with a much shorter history than the districts mentioned earlier. As with their United States sisters, much of the early history wasn't written in secretary's ledgers. To their credit, within the past five years each province has written a complete history of the women's groups, and the Canadian Conference Women in Mission has done the same. Considering that many of the originators of the groups are still living, or at least known to persons associated with the groups today, the Canadian WM groups have produced a valuable historical record.

British Columbia was the first to organize on provincial level in 1939, Saskatchewan followed in 1943, Manitoba in 1944, Ontario in 1947, Alberta in 1948, and Southwest Ontario in 1967. The Canadian Conference Women's

Missionary Association organized formally in 1952 in Manitoba. In her talk at the twenty-fifth anniversary of that occasion, former President Mary Harder said, "The organization is comparatively young. Our pioneering women assisted by some men put a lot of effort, understanding, wisdom, good judgment, farsightedness, vision, tenderness, love, dream, and sometimes a lot of gumption and common sense into forming this organization." She spoke about the inherent desire for independence that characterized local groups and which is also evident in the letters of the General Conference Executive Committee. She added, "More women from other provinces as well as from the hosting province attended the women's conference. . . . They saw that their individual rights of their local societies and their provincial conferences were not lost. Much more could be achieved in a united effort. Love and trust and a sense of belonging became firmly established." [29]

Both programs and personal contact with missionaries, many of whom come from Canada, have always had strong emphasis. Because of the great distances between groups in Canada, women meet only once a year as a Canadian WM organization, but in each province at least one meeting a year, and often two, are held. The year 1977 marked the twenty-fifth anniversary year of the official organization of Canadian Conference WM, and it was fittingly celebrated with a program of praise and thanksgiving at Toronto. Their *History of Canadian Women in Mission* was prepared for this special commemorative year.

Sister Hillegonda van der Smissen reports the first program given in what is now Western District was patterned after the kind given in Middle District. The General Conference met at the Alexanderwohl Church in Kansas in 1896 and the women were responsible for the mission festival, a new procedure in this area. Sister Hillegonda writes that there were mixed feelings about the program originally, but when the time for the program came there was standing room only, and some people who couldn't find seats drove their carriages under the open windows of the country church to hear. "It was needless to worry whether a women's missionary program might find objectors here, on the contrary it was most favorably received." [30]

The first program given for mission society members only at Western Dictrict Conference was in 1923, although by 1900 there were already fourteen societies in existence. The earliest minutes of Western District WM are unfortunately lost, but, based on reporting in *Missionary News and Notes*, the group organized as a women's missionary organization in 1930 at Alexanderwohl and held its first meeting "in the open on the sunny side of the large church." [31] The first local women's group was organized at Halstead, Kansas, in 1881.

One unique experience of Western District Women in Mission concerns their spring meetings which have been bus tours to areas of district home missions. These were enthusiastically received as a means of learning more about the district's outreach, and as friendly get-togethers for the 78 to 230 women who took part each time.

According to the *Handbook of Information* of the General Conference, only the presidents of the Western District Women in Mission, Ontario WM, and southwest Ontario WM are on the executive councils of their district or province.

A statistical picture of Women in Mission at the end of 1979 shows the following:

Canadian Conference	4,456 members	207 groups
Central District	1,086 "	45 "
Eastern District	543 "	24 "
Northern District	1,061 "	32 "
Pacific District	521 "	27 "
Western District	2,234 "	82 "
Totals	9,901 members	417 groups [32]

When Metta Moyer of the Central District was Young Mission Worker adviser in 1965, she made an analysis of the local scene in a letter to the Executive Committee. (The dots are hers and do not indicate omissions; presumably they represented long pauses for thought.) Metta wrote, "My experience is that the busiest women are among the best local workers . . . and many churches make delegates only out of their pastors . . . or long time deacons . . . so that few actually of busy lay women get to come out . . . due to double service as mothers and personal employment, or due to such factors. We are living in an 'escalating economy' that pressurizes all into its changing moods . . . and our church must do its best to work in that atmosphere, too."[33]

8 tomorrow

What of tomorrow? Has the day for women's mission organizations run its course? Almost a century and a half has gone by since Mennonite women first met in Ohio to form a mission society. What is to determine whether such groups have validity in the future?

The president of Women in Mission spoke of that organization in 1979 as being "in transition," [1] which implies going from one point to a different place. The original emphasis came from women who found most of their time and talents utilized within their homes, but who still felt the need to be supportive of the mission outreach of the church and each other. Today's crowded schedules take away from home time, and modern conveniences replace hours of labor once needed by the provider. Motels and hotels reduce the guest lists in homes. Telephone conversations replace face-to-face discussions and leisurely conversation. *Heathen* is an outmoded term, and partnership in mission is much different than giver-receiver relationships.

The membership of Women in Mission has remained relatively stable. However, it is of grave concern that many of its members are older women whose ranks are not being filled by younger ones. How large must an organization be to be effective? Employment of women outside their homes is a factor affecting mission groups that must be considered, as is the need of workers to keep what few hours that remain a family affair. The need for "realism and adaptability" is a sobering imperative called for by a former officer. [2]

On the positive side are the rewarding international relationships possible when the sponsoring group is large enough and strong enough to promote such contacts. The need to be supportive of women and their families as structures change is ever present, perhaps even more so today than when one's sphere was smaller. There are services called for within the church and community that are best carried out when there are persons organized and ready to be of assistance, and although this is an age of individualism, there is still a strength that numbers can provide. Women's organizations, although seldom promoted for that reason, are acknowledged training centers for fuller participation in church and conference, and when the local church and conference open to more utilization of abilities, the need will increase rather than decrease. As mission strategies and direction change, and personal relationships continue to assume greater importance than physical plant, the need for women to be a part of that relationship will grow also.

It was easier to assess the contributions of women when you counted garments sewed, quilts and comforters provided, and dollars sent. How does one measure personal growth, moral backing, the representation of women and women's concerns to the church, support of conference, leadership training, the worth of international relationships, and acts of service and kindness in congregation and community? If women's mission groups cease, what of greater worth will take their place?

notes

Chapter 1

[1] Letter from Agnes Wiens to the Executive Committee, April 4, 1918, Women's Missionary Association Correspondence/Alphabetical Subjects folder 2, Mennonite Library and Archives, Bethel College, North Newton, Kansas (cited hereafter as MLA).

[2] November 19, 1924, Women's Association folder 45, MLA.

[3] Taken from "India Missionaries," biographies published by the Women's Home and Foreign Missionary Association, March 1949, MLA.

[4] Letter written May 19, 1947, Women's Association folder 68, MLA.

[5] *The Mennonite*, September 27, 1917, p. 4.

[6] *Ibid.*, January 30, 1919, p. 5.

[7] *Ibid.*

[8] Bill Block term paper: "A study on the Auxiliary Committees of the General Conference Mennonite Church," January 1957, Chicago. MLA.

[9] Letter to Executive Committee, October 7, 1921, Women's Association folder 6, MLA.

[10] This term is used by Susannah in a letter to Executive Committee, September 27, 1920, Women's Association folder 5, MLA.

[11] Letter to Executive Committee, October 27, 1920, Women's Association folder 5, MLA.

[12] Letter to Executive Committee, November 22, 1920, Women's Association folder 5, MLA.

[13] Letter to Executive Committee, July 9, 1924, Women's Association folder 45, MLA.

[14] Goerz, June 17, 1924, Women's Association folder 45, MLA.

[15] Haury, June 19, 1932, Women's Association folder 49, MLA.

[16] Goerz, January 14, 1925, Women's Association folder 46, MLA.

[17] *Missionary News and Notes*, February 1931, p. 1. (cited hereafter as *MNN*).

[18] August 26, 1920, Women's Missionary Societies triennial report.

[19] Goerz, November 18, 1924, Women's Association folder 86, MLA.

[20] Agnes Wiens, April 4, 1918, Women's Association folder 2, MLA.

[21] Haury, November 12, 1924, Women's Association folder 86, MLA.

[22] *MNN*, October 1926, unpaged.

[23] Letter from P. A. Penner in which he quotes Martha's response to the gift of fruit he had sent in behalf of the mission societies. *The Mennonite*, July 25, 1918.

[24] *Ibid.*

[25] Conversation of the author with David Habegger.

[26] "A Timely Missionary Talk" given by Sara Schultz at Bluffton, Ohio, in 1951. Copy provided by her daughter, Lora Oyer.

[27] Letter from Haury to Mrs. S. M. Musselman, May 19, 1935, Women's Association folder 158, MLA.

[28] Petter to committee, June 15, 1931, Women's Association folder 13, MLA.

[29] James C. Juhnke, *A People of Mission* (Newton, Kansas: Faith and Life Press, 1979), p. 35.

[30] *MNN*, November 1929, unpaged.

[31] Martha R. Penner letter to Executive Committee, July 9, 1926, Women's Association folder 87, MLA.

[32] These figures were taken from a history of "The Women's Missionary Association" written for the Diamond Jubilee Conference 1935.

[33] *MNN*, December 1926, unpaged.

[34] Laura Petter had written a letter to the Executive Committee, August 17, 1930, in which she pleaded for no additional sewed items to be sent to the Indians. The WMA president, Martha Kaufman, penciled a note on the top of Laura's letter which she sent to her committee, in which she talked about the need for more than sewing. Folder 12, MLA.

[35] Boehr, letter to Executive Committee, March 31, 1919. Women's Missionary Association folder 3, MLA.

[36] The constitution was changed in 1974, but in council sessions this was accorded earlier. A travel pool for advisers had been provided in 1970.

[37] Women's Missionary Association Committee and Council minutes, July 2, 1952.

Chapter 2

[1] Sister Hillegonda van der Smissen, *The History of Missionary Societies* (Literature Committee of the Women's Home and Foreign Missionary Association, undated), p. 12.

[2] "Home Missions," a brochure published by the Literature Committee of the Women's Home and Foreign Missionary Association, 1941), p. 14.

[3] WMA Ledger Book 1927-29.

[4] *Ibid.*

[5] "Home Missions," p. 12.

[6] *MNN*, September 1927, unpaged.

[7] *MNN*, March 1928, unpaged.

[8] July 29, 1932, Women's Association folder 89, MLA.

[9] *MNN*, December 1935, p. 4.

[10] WMA minutes, triennial session 1933.

[11] *MNN*, October 1938, p. 2.

[12] *MNN*, April 1931, p. 2.

[13] *MNN*, September 1941, p. 1.

[14] WMA Executive Committee minutes, June 18, 1943.

[15] Matilda Voth, August 2, 1943, Women's Association folder 63, MLA.

[16] 1947 Triennium Report of the WMA Executive Committee and Council minutes.

[17]*MNN*, May 1946, pages 11-12.

[18]Letter from Mary Burkhart to Martha Goerz, April 29, 1943, Women's Association folder 180, MLA. This letter spells out the Christmas note referred to.

[19]Matilda Voth, January 20, 1944, Women's Association folder 181, MLA.

[20]Letter to Emma Ruth, June 23, 1943, Women's Association folder 180, MLA.

[21]Letter April 26, 1943, Women's Association folder 180, MLA.

[22]Burkhart, undated letter, Women's Association folder 134, MLA.

[23]Letter to committee August 9, 1944, Women's Association folder 181, MLA.

[24]Letter from Neuenschwander, February 14, 1947, Women's Association folder 102, MLA.

[25]Letter dated July 12, 1946, Women's Association folder 181, MLA.

[26]Letter dated February 3, 1946, Women's Association folder 181, MLA.

[27]Letter from Neuenschwander June 9, 1951, to Mrs. Eldon Graber, WMA secretary, Women's Association folder 183, MLA.

[28]Eleanor Camp, August 25, 1951, Women's Association folder 208, MLA.

[29]Letter from Rev. J. J. Plenert, July 7, 1947, Women's Association folder 102, MLA.

[30]Letter from Neuenschwander May 21, 1947, Women's Association folder 102, MLA.

[31]*Ibid.*, July 27, 1950.

[32]Matilda Voth, February 26, 1945, Women's Association folder 102, MLA.

[33]1947 Report of the Visitation Program, minutes of the WMA.

[34]Conversation of author and Matilda Voth, October 26, 1979.

Chapter 3

[1]Martha Burkhalter, "The Conversion of Garib," a brochure published by the Literature Committee of the Women's Missionary Society, 1925.

[2]*MNN*, November 1937, p. 1.

[3]Wilhelmena Kuyf, "Internment Echoes," p. 1.

[4]*MNN*, May 1947, unpaged.

[5]*MNN*, July 1947, p. 8.

[6]"Guide to Mission Study," 1972/73. (Literature Committee of the Women's Missionary Association), Part 2, Session 6, p. 33.

[7]*MNN*, October 1926, unpaged.

[8]Letter from F. Luella Krehbiel to Executive Committee, December 10, 1929, Women's Association folder 11, MLA.

[9]*MNN*, April, 1936, p. 3.

[10]Letter dated August 12, 1947, Women's Association folder 184, MLA.

[11]*MNN*, November 1946, p. 13.

[12]*MNN*, November 1946, June 1938, June 1937.

[13]*MNN*, April 1935, page 3 (bilingual issue).

[14]*MNN*, October 1926, unpaged.

[15]Interview with Joanna Andres, July 6, 1979.

[16] Recommendation IV by the Executive Committee to triennial session 1945.

[17] Eleanor Camp in letter dated February 9, 1951, Women's Association folder 125, MLA.

[18] Letter from Harriet Dyck, January 1, 1960, Women's Association folder 145, MLA.

[19] Eleanor Camp to Harriet Dyck, February 8, 1960, Women's Association folder 145, MLA.

[20] West Zion Mission Workers, Moundridge, Kansas. Reported in "They Saw the Necessity," a history of Western District mission societies in 1935.

[21] Eleanor Camp, January 7, 1948, Women's Association folder 125, MLA.

[22] Highlights from a letter from Sara Schultz were summarized to the committee by Secretary Matilda Voth on October 11, 1939, Women's Association folder 125, MLA.

[23] *Ibid.*

[24] Anecdote told by Vinora Salzman. Submitted by Olga Martens.

[25] Conversation with the author and Tillie Jantzen.

[26] Eleanor Camp to Stella Kreider, January 31, 1948, Women's Association folder 26, MLA.

[27] Stella Kreider's paper "Cooperation Among Mennonite Women," presented at WMA meeting June 4, 1945, WMA minutes of triennial sessions.

[28] Cc of letter to Bethel College by Bennie Bargen dated August 19, 1949, Women's Association folder 126, MLA.

[29] *Window to Mission*, April 1974, p. W-2.

Chapter 4

[1] *MNN*, February 1931, unpaged.

[2] Unpublished history of First Mennonite Ladies Aid Society of Allentown, Pennsylvania, provided by Viola Weidner.

[3] *History of British Columbia Women in Mission*, 1976, p. 23.

[4] Information provided by Isolde Loewen, B.C. Women in Mission treasurer, October 9, 1979.

[5] Report by Mrs. A. B. Reimer at the twenty-fifth commemoration of the Hoffnungsau Church, Inman, Kansas, provided by her daughter, Olga Martens.

[6] Marie Lohrentz in her report of the visitation program in 1947. Minutes of Executive Committee and Council of the Women's Missionary Association.

[7] Unpublished history of West Swamp, Quakertown, Pennsylvania, mission society, provided by Elsie Stenson.

[8] *MNN*, March 1928, unpaged.

[9] Minutes of the Missionary Society of the Alberta Community Church, Portland, Oregon, January 9, 1930, provided by Edith B. Haack.

[10] Letter dated December 9, 1925, Women's Association folder 86, MLA.

[11] Interview by the author with Dorothea Dyck, June 6, 1979. Dorothea was a strong promoter of the whole mission program and, like Frieda Regier Entz, not of "specials" only.

122

[12] Marie Lohrentz to Executive Committee.

[13] Marie Lohrentz's letter to the Executive Committee after her visit in Saskatchewan, July 19, 1946.

[14] *History of Canadian Women in Mission*, 1977, p. 2.

[15] Aganetha Fast's report of her itineration in Ontario, 1946, WMA Executive Committee and Council minutes.

[16] Mrs. G. A. Krehbiel, letter written March 12, 1948, Women's Association folder 58, MLA.

[17] *Ibid.*

[18] Eleanor Camp to Mrs. G. A. Krehbiel, May 17, 1954. Women's Association folder 59, MLA.

[19] Minutes of the Executive Committee and Council, December 7-9, 1957.

[20] Information given by Vinora Salzman, provided by Olga Martens.

[21] Letter, June 23, 1947, Women's Association folder 58, MLA.

[22] Letter, October 13, 1971.

[23] Letter, October 18, 1971.

[24] Letter to author from Helen Kruger, March 8, 1979.

[25] Letter to author from Betty Epp, July 27, 1979.

[26] Letter to author from Naomi Lehman, September 28, 1979.

[27] General Conference Board of Trustees files.

[28] Marie Lohrentz, April 2, 1952, Women's Association folder 91, MLA.

[29] Martha Graber, WMA secretary, April 3, 1952, Women's Association folder 91, MLA.

[30] Marie Lohrentz, letter May 29, 1952, Women's Association folder 91, MLA.

[31] General Conference Board of Trustees files.

[32] Letter from Mrs. A. J. Richert, April 22, 1947, Women's Association folder 130, MLA.

[33] *Women in Mission Manual Supplement*, 1979, p. 10.

Chapter 5

[1] Executive Committee and Council minutes December 1-2, 1950.

[2] *Ibid.*, December 5, 1959, letter from P. K. Regier explaining the board's nine-point memo.

[3] Summary of Mission Board - WMA discussion at Chicago. WMA Executive Committee and Council minutes.

[4] *Ibid.*, Eleanor Camp, July 13, 1960.

[5] Letter to Executive Committee, September 27, 1920, Women's Association folder 5, MLA.

[6] January 10, 1947, Women's Association folder 164, MLA.

[7] Letter from Rev. Nyce, January 25, 1947, Women's Association folder 164, MLA.

[8] Marie Lohrentz, January 28, 1947, Women's Association folder 164, MLA.

[9] Marie Lohrentz, November 24, 1951, Women's Association folder 91, MLA.

[10] Eleanor Camp to Marianna Habegger, November 12, 1959.

[11] President's Report, 1974 Council of Commissions Report Book, p. 2.

[12] *WMA Manual*, 1968, p. 45.

[13] Letter from Mrs. C. E. Rediger, June 10, 1947, Women's Association folder 65 MLA.

[14] Marie Lohrentz, October 14, 1947, Women's Association folder 66, MLA.

[15] Eleanor Camp, May 4, 1956, Women's Association folder 99, MLA.

[16] *MNN*, February 1972, p. 10, "First Women's Delegation to Congo."

[17] Mary Harder, talk given in Toronto, 1977, at the twenty-fifth anniversary of Canadian Women in Mission.

[18] *MNN*, August 1971, p. 13.

[19] *Ibid.*, p. 4.

[20] Margaret Ewert's report, Council of Commissions Report Book, 1979.

[21] Letter to James Bertsche, AIMM, April 6, 1979.

[22] *MNN*, October 1933, p. 3.

[23] Letter to Hulda Meyers, September 30, 1940, Women's Association folder 111, MLA.

[24] *MNN*, March 1935, p. 3.

[25] *Leaders' Resource Manual for Young Mission Workers* (Newton, Kansas: Faith and Life Press, 1965), p. 19.

[26] *Missions Today*, February 1968, p. 18.

[27] WM Advisory Council Reports, February 1979, Young Mission Workers Report.

Chapter 6

[1] *Persons Becoming Packet:* MCC Task Force on Women, April 1974. Report of Women's Caucus, December 6, 1972, NCCUSA.

[2] Minutes of WMA Executive Council, February 8, 1973.

[3] Minutes of WMA Executive Committee, June 25-27, 1973, p. 5.

[4] *Ibid.*

[5] WMA Executive Council Reports, February 1974.

[6] *Ibid.*

[7] WM Advisory Council Reports, February 1977.

[8] *Window to Mission*, July 1974, p. W-2.

[9] WMA Executive Council Reports, February 1973.

[10] February 7, 1977.

[11] Letter to Advisory Council from Joan Wiebe, October 5, 1977.

[12] Women in Mission Advisory Council Reports, February 1978.

[13] Leah Sonwani directs General Conference work with women in India and acted as hostess for General Conference guests at the All-India women's conference.

[14] WM Advisory Council Reports, February 1978.

[15] *Window to Mission*, March/April 1978, p. W-14.

[16] Copy of letter to Mary Anne Boschman, November 10, 1976.

[17] *Window to Mission*, October/November 1978, p. W-14, Joan Wiebe.

[18] Letter from the Taichung Women's Choir to Women in Mission, September 1, 1978. Reprinted in 1979 manual insert.

[19] Executive Committee minutes, September 1979.

[20] *Ibid.*

124

Chapter 7

[1] Trinity Church women's groups, Hillsboro, Kansas. Information provided by Dora Bartel.

[2] Unpublished history of Ladies Mission Society, Hereford Mennonite Church, Bally, Pennsylvania.

[3] Pannabecker, S. F., *Faith in Ferment* (Newton, Kansas: Faith and Life Press, 1968), p. 78.

[4] *Ibid.*, p. 105.

[5] Naomi Lehman, "Outstretched Hands," p. 2. Pageant presented at the 1959 triennial session.

[6] *Centennial Chronicle 1978*, First Mennonite Church of Christian, Moundridge, Kansas (Mennonite Press, North Newton, Kans.), p. 6.

[7] Albena Deckert, a report prepared for the seventy-fifth anniversary of Salem Zion Church, Freeman, South Dakota.

[8] Unpublished history of King's Daughters, Alexanderwohl Church, Goessel, Kansas. Information provided by Mrs. Ferd Duerksen.

[9] Information provided by Elda Bachman relating to First Mennonite Church, Newton, Kansas, mission societies.

[10] Unpublished history of Menno Church Society, Ritzville, Washington, provided by Phyllis Franz.

[11] *SWM*, a History of Saskatchewan Women in Mission, 1977, p. 79.

[12] Unpublished history of First Mennonite Church societies, Aberdeen, Idaho, provided by Elma Linscheid.

[13] Rachel Kreider's report on the history of First Mennonite Church, Wadsworth, Ohio, mission society.

[14] "A Review of the Hebron Mission Workers" by Mrs. Sam Regier, December 1951.

[15] *Centennial Chronicle*, p. 6.

[16] Letter to Anna Isaac, September 13, 1919, Women's Association folder 3, MLA.

[17] Hilda Janzen, 1963 Adviser's Report to the WMA Council.

[18] Unpublished historical sketch of the Ladies Aid Society of the First Mennonite Church, Allentown, Pennsylvania, provided by Viola Weidner.

[19] *SWM*, a History of Saskatchewan Women in Mission, 1977, p. 37.

[20] Historical Survey and Statistical Report of the Women's Missionary Societies of the Northern District Conference, 1935.

[21] *Ontario Women in Mission*, p. 14.

[22] *History of Manitoba Women in Mission*, p. 76, 1977.

[23] Pannabecker, S. F. *Faith in Ferment*, pp. 105-6.

[24] *Ibid.*, p. 304.

[25] Minutes of the thirteenth Pacific District Conference, June 14-17, 1908, resolution 6.

[26] May 25, 1933, Women's Association folder 89, MLA.

[27] Mrs. Sam Preheim, report pp. 4-5, of *Bericht und Referate der Nördlichen Distrikt Konferenz*, 1926.

[28] "Heritage Highlights," published by WMA 1977.

[29] Talk given at Toronto, 1977, "My Involvement with the Canadian Women in Mission 1966-72."

[30] Sister Hillegonda van der Smissen, *The History of Our Mission Societies*, pp. 29-30.

[31] *MNN*, January 1931.

[32] Women in Mission Advisory Council Report Book, February 1980.

[33] Metta Moyer, letter to Dorothea Dyck, February 19, 1965.

Chapter 8

[1] Lora Oyer, president of Women in Mission, Executive Committee minutes September 6-7, 1979.

[2] Rachel Kreider, former Central District officer, letter to author, June 20, 1979.

acknowledgements

We wish to express our thanks to the following people and mission groups who contributed information and assistance for this history:

Lora Oyer, Helen Friesen, Phyllis Baumgartner, Nina Roupp, Romaine Sprunger, Naomi Lehman, Helen Kruger, Naomi Wollmann, Norma Wiens, Mary Valencia, Margot Fieguth, Ruth Epp, Betty Epp, Suzanne Tiessen, Dorothy A. Krehbiel, Dorothea J. Dyck, Lydia Ewert, Rachel W. Kreider, Robert Kreider, Elda Bachman, Helen Regier, Huldah Friesen, Joanna Andres, Matilda Voth, Hilda Janzen, David Habegger, Marie Dyck, Margaret Goerzen, Mary Harder, Phyllis Franz, Jeanette Harnly, Elma Linscheid, Olga Martens, Mrs. Erwin E. Schrag, Isolde Loewen, Bertha Peters, Albena Deckert, Helen Coon, Mariam Schmidt, Helen Rempel, Rosella Toevs.

First Mennonite, Reedley, California: Ellen J. Ewy, Luise Philipp.
Alexanderwohl, Goessel, Kansas: Mrs. Anton Schmidt, Mrs. Ferd Duerksen.
Hebron, Buhler, Kansas: Gladys Regier.
Menno, Ritzville, Washington: Bertha Franz, Agatha Franz, Phyllis Franz, Dorothy Franz.
Trinity, Hillsboro, Kansas: Mrs. Arnold Penner, Mrs. Walter Gaede, Dora Bartel (including the histories of Johannestal and Brudertal churches).
Bethany, Quakertown, Pennsylvania: Edna Detweiler.

First, Allentown, Pennsylvania: Viola Weidner and four friends.

First, Phoenix, Arizona: Carolyn Yost.

Lorraine Avenue, Wichita, Kansas: Rosa Kaufman.

Lower Skippack, Creamery, Pennsylvania: Estella Keyser.

First, Aberdeen, Idaho: Mrs. Dan Wenger, Catherine Harder, Marie Neuman, Elsie Klempel, Anna Wiebe.

Hereford, Bally, Pennsylvania: Mae Latshaw.

Zion, Souderton, Pennsylvania: Edna Z. Guhl.

Alberta Community (Peace), Portland, Oregon: Edith B. Haack.

Indian Valley, Harleysville, Pennsylvania: Louise Hagin.

Church of the Good Samaritan, Holland, Pennsylvania: Alberta Bergey.

Eden, Schwenksville, Pennsylvania, L. May Markley.

First, Paso Robles, California: Emily Toevs.

West Swamp, Quakertown, Pennsylvania: Elsie Stenson.

Glendale, Lynden, Washington: Wilma Warkentin.

Calvary, Aurora, Oregon: Nina Roupp.

Grace, Dallas, Oregon.

First, Upland, California: Jerry Boshart.

Community Church, Fresno, California: Verna Epp.

The records of Canadian societies were provided in these histories:
The History of Canadian Mennonite Women in Mission
Alberta Women in Mission
History of British Columbia Women in Mission
Manitoba Women in Mission
SWM (Saskatchewan Women in Mission)
The Story of Women in Mission - Southwest Ontario
Ontario Women in Mission

My special thanks are due Joan Wiebe, Jeannette Schmidt, Ruth Unrau, Jeannie Zehr, and Robert Kreider who gave extra help and friendly encouragement.

Gladys Goering